WAY *of*

Psychic Protection

In the same series:

Thorsons WAY *of* **Chakras**
Caroline Shola Arewa

Thorsons WAY *of* **Crystal Healing**
Ronald Bonewitz

Thorsons WAY *of* **Meditation**
Christina Feldman

Thorsons WAY *of* **NLP**
Joseph O'Connor and Ian McDermott

Thorsons WAY *of* **Natural Magic**
Nigel Pennick

Thorsons WAY *of* **Reiki**
Kajsa Krishni Boräng

Thorsons WAY *of* **Reincarnation**
Judy Hall

Thorsons WAY *of* **Tarot**
Evelyne Herbin and Terry Donaldson

Thorsons WAY *of* **Tibetan Buddhism**
Lama Jampa Thaye

Thorsons WAY *of* **Wicca**
Vivianne Crowley

Thorsons WAY *of* **Zen**
Martine Batchelor

WAY *of* Psychic Protection

Judy Hall

Author of *The Crystal Bible*

Thorsons

Thorsons
An Imprint of HarperCollins*Publishers*
77–85 Fulham Palace Road
Hammersmith, London W6 8JB
The website address is: www.thorsonselement.com

First published by Thorsons as *Principles of Psychic Protection* 1999
This edition published by Thorsons 2001

13 15 14 12

© Judy Hall 1999, 2001

Judy Hall asserts the moral right to be
identified as the author of this work

A catalogue record for this book
is available from the British Library

ISBN-13 978-0-00-711021-6
ISBN-10 0-00-711021-9

Printed and bound in Great Britain by
Martins the Printers Limited, Berwick upon Tweed

All rights reserved. No part of this publication may be
reproduced, stored in a retrieval system, or transmitted,
in any form or by any means, electronic, mechanical,
photocopying, recording or otherwise, without the prior
permission of the publishers.

Contents

Acknowledgements

I would like to thank David Eastoe, Dawn Robins and David Lawson for case material included within this book, Danny Dawson and Jo Neary for acupuncture information, and Victor Sims for his Computer Clear programme. As always my partner Robert Jacobs provided invaluable help.

ABOUT THE Author

Astrologer and karmic counsellor, **Judy Hall** was trained in psychic protection by the late Christine Hartley (Dion Fortune's literary agent and Western-mystery tradition colleague). Judy has run psychic development groups for over twenty-five years. She is a workshop-leader for The College of Psychic Studies in London and has taught psychic protection all over the world. She is the author of twelve books including *Principles of Past Life Therapy*, *Hands Across Time: the Soulmate Enigma* and *Deja Who? A New Look at Past Lives.*

Foreword

A Personal Note by David Lawson

Good psychic protection needs to be viewed in a positive light and implemented with the regularity of an effective health regime. As with all good health care, prevention is better than cure but a first-aid kit and some practical tips are always useful. There is much that we can all do to protect and empower ourselves in the absence of expert help.

When we do need expert advice and assistance we can do no better than to consult Judy Hall. Judy has an extraordinary wealth of skills borne out of many years experience and a natural intuitive ability that is quite exceptional. What is more, she is one of the most thorough and determined practitioners that I have ever encountered. I have known Judy to persist until all the threads of a problem have been found and carefully unravelled. Indeed, she has often brought effective completion to karmic healing work that has been ineffectively instigated by other, less skilled therapists.

With *Way of Psychic Protection*, Judy offers us both an effective tool kit for our own protection and a comprehensive introduction to an area of specialist healing work that caters for universal human need. Good psychic protection is not about feeding human fears and superstitions. Rather it is concerned with improving the quality of our lives and promoting healthy relationships.

As a spiritual healer and teacher of personal development courses I encounter issues of psychic invasion on a regular basis. Methods of psychic clearing and effective protection have become an integral part of my work. I have also observed a powerful link between those problems and patterns of belief that we may have learnt from childhood. Beliefs in evil, beliefs in a punishing god, superstitious beliefs, victim mentality, self-punishing beliefs and issues of low self-esteem can all make us more available for psychic interference. In addressing these issues it is always comforting to know that I can call upon the expertise of Judy Hall, a specialist with great practical ability and a woman of compassion and extraordinary talent.

David Lawson is an author, healer, spiritual teacher and broadcaster. His books include *How to Develop Your Sixth Sense* and *Principles of Self-healing* (Thorsons), *An Oracle of Ancient Egypt – The Eye of Horus* (Connections) and *A Company of Angels* (Findhorn Press).

Introduction

Psychic Protection

If you have picked up this book, you may be wondering what psychic protection is and whether you need it. On the other hand, you may be in need of psychic protection and looking for ways to safeguard yourself. Psychic protection acts as an impermeable barrier to other people's thoughts and feelings. It keeps out unwanted intrusions and prevents energy leakage. It safeguards your inner – and outer – space. Psychic protection is subtle and invisible. It is a defensive screen around you, a cocoon within which you are safe. Psychic protection is putting out, and attracting back, only good vibrations. Practising psychic protection strengthens your aura. It creates a natural defence mechanism, the equivalent of your physical immune system. Practising psychic self-defence gives a psychic immunoguard.

Psychic Protection

Creating a safe space around yourself, screening out unwanted thoughts and feelings from, and preventing energy loss to, other people or places.

As more people seek to open up their consciousness or develop their intuitive and psychic or healing abilities, so the need for clear, simple guidelines to psychic protection increases. As more people undertake shamanic journeys, so the need to protect oneself at the subtle level is greater than ever. However, almost everyone at some time in their life will need psychic protection.

One of the best ways to protect yourself is not to be fearful. As we shall see, fear attracts negative energies and so you have to do extra work to create a safe space for yourself. Many of the experiences described in this book are 'worst case scenarios' and hopefully you will never have to deal with them. But if you do, then you will know how to protect yourself.

> ## *Psychic*
>
> 1 *The subtle, unseen realm tuned into by a 'sixth sense' that picks up thoughts, feelings and atmospheres from outside oneself. 'Being psychic' means that you are in contact with this realm.*
> 2 *Operating at the level of the psyche – can be rational or irrational, conscious or unconscious.*

Psychic Pitfalls

People who work with other people, especially in counselling or healing, are particularly susceptible to picking up negative energies or 'thought forms' from their clients. You need a quick way to release these, and a form of protection which will prevent them from attaching in the first place.

Thought Forms

An entity or object that exists on the lower astral and which was brought into being by the power of thought, or of belief. Concentration on an idea, or a fear, can produce a thought form. For instance, a god could be said to be a thought form, as could a demonic being.

If you are a counsellor or healer, without psychic protection your own energy may be drained by your clients. There are 'psychic vampires' around and needy people are the most likely to sap your energy. You may unknowingly take home your clients' thoughts and feelings. You may be prone to illness and feel depleted without realizing that this comes from a psychic source connected to your work.

Even if you do not work professionally with people's feelings and energies, you may still be a 'psychic hoover' soaking up the feelings and emanations of places and people.

Psychic Vampires

People who draw in energy from other people to feed their own energy. Vampirism is sucking or leeching energy from another person. This can happen on a psychic, emotional or mental level.

Psychic Hoover

Someone who absorbs, and is harmed by, energy, emotions, feelings and impressions from another person or place.

If you are psychically over-sensitive, a simple journey into work is fraught with problems. Sit next to someone who has a headache, and you arrive at work with a headache yourself. Stand crushed up against someone who is angry and you absorb that anger. Emanations can sometimes affect even the most psychically insensitive. Sleep in a strange hotel room, and you share the bed with everyone else who has ever slept there. Not everything left behind in such rooms is physical and easily cleared away. Places too can affect you. Stand on a geopathically-stressed spot, and your energy rushes out of your feet. As nature abhors a vacuum, something else will rush in to fill the space.

Geopathic Stress

Geopathic stress is created by electro-magnetic radiation, ley lines, underground streams and such like. It is often known as 'sick building syndrome'. It can adversely affect the immune system as well as the body's innate psychic protection. It may attract non-physical entities – 'ghosts' – or hold impressions of previous events.

The Aura

The multi-layered, luminous subtle energy field that surrounds your physical body.

Many people are surprised to find that their psychic energy is being affected by someone, or something, attached to their aura – a condition known as Psychic Attachment. This 'other person' may be alive or dead. They are often family members who have not moved on after death but they can also be someone with whom there has been a contact a long time ago and who has been forgotten about – at a conscious level. Equally the hold can be by a still living ex-partner who finds it impossible to let go, or by a mother who cannot release her children. Such an attachment can only take place where personal boundaries are weak, where there is an energy gap, or where the family was psychically enmeshed. Detaching such a soul and moving them on their way can be most beneficial for both parties. The 'something' that is attached or influencing may be a thought form or a mental influence from another person, alive or dead.

Psychic Attachment

Another person or being, alive or dead, adversely influencing someone through an auric attachment. Objects can also be the subject of psychic attachment. Thought forms can attach psychically to people or objects.

Some people have the misfortune to come under deliberate psychic attack by someone who is angry, jealous, or bears a grudge. If this is the case, then you need to learn how to protect your space and those around you – and you may have to learn how to return the energy to its source. The key is to know when this is appropriate and when withdrawing your attention altogether would be a more effective form of defence.

Psychic Attack

The intentional or unwitting focussing or harnessing of psychic or mental energies to bring harm to another person.

Protecting Yourself

The key to good psychic protection is to find exactly the right method for you and the situations you find yourself in. Something you can use quickly and easily. You need a method in harmony with your own way of thinking. A practice that resonates with what you yourself believe. Something that feels good. You will find many possibilities in the pages that follow. Practising a few now will help you to select the one that feels right for you. Perfecting the technique allows you to use it when you need it – it is no help at all to have to hunt for the book when you become aware of a problem. Your method of protection needs to be well established so that it becomes an automatic process to switch it on *before it is needed*. Indeed, many people find that starting and ending the day by checking that their protection is in place gives them a feeling of safety that nothing can shake.

Good Vibrations

We are surrounded by a host of unseen vibrations, a field of invisible energies, many of which can subtly affect our sense of well-being – and our ability to protect ourselves psychically. If your own energetic vibrations are balanced and in harmony, if your outlook is positive and life-enhancing, then you have a natural protection. The less in touch with everyday reality you are, the more tenuous your hold on the physical world, and the more ungrounded you become, the greater the chance of picking up something nasty or of having your energy leeched. The more fearful you are, with ingrained negative thought patterns, the more opportunity your own fears have to turn on you.

The best protection of all is being well-grounded, rooted comfortably in everyday life with your feet firmly on the ground. You can hold 'way-out' views and undertake esoteric tasks, but if you are 'down-to-earth' then you will naturally protect yourself. How well grounded you are in your physical body will affect how easily other people can penetrate your defences. With only a toehold in incarnation, and hazy boundaries, you will be wide open to invasion. It is like having a beacon shining out of the top of your head advertising 'room to let' or 'free energy source'. Shallow breathing too invites psychic penetration. Grounding and anchoring work at the physical level, with some good deep breaths into the belly, is essential before any psychic work is undertaken.

Psychic Penetration

Energy, thoughts or feelings from another person passing through the body's natural defences and causing harm or energy depletion.

Being grounded sends out the right signals: 'I am at home in my body and my energy is intact – and will stay that way.' So too does knowing yourself well, and accepting the dark corners of your psyche just as much as the bright ones. Then there are no repressed secret parts of yourself to rise up and, seemingly, 'attack' you from outside. Being in control of your thought processes gives out 'good vibrations' and it is as well to remember that, in the psychic world, like attracts like.

Attitude of mind affects how well you are protected. If you are positive and have good vibrations, you will be much stronger than someone who constantly thinks negative thoughts and gives off 'bad vibes'. What we put out comes back. What we fear we attract. What we believe in, we bring into being. So, visualization is a powerful tool for creating a safe space. Affirmations can change an ingrained pattern of thought, attracting more constructive situations. So too does a positive outlook. If you are constantly fearful, then you create an unsafe space. What you most fear will be drawn towards you. If you let go of the trepidation, you will lose the fear and free yourself from the possibility.

Visualization

Using 'mind pictures' to bring things into being. A powerful tool for protection and for creating change.

Psychic Solutions

Within these pages you will find visualizations to enhance your natural psychic protection. Simple daily rituals can support you in breaking old patterns. So too can crystals and talismans – which have been used for this purpose for thousands of years. A modern method of protection uses Flower Essences – subtle, vibrational energies that resonate with the aura to strengthen it and to cleanse the space around you. The essence Ti (Fes and Aloha), for instance, lifts curses and helps to release astral possession. Flower Essences also gently change negative thought patterns and emotions into positive, life affirming expectations. At the end of the sections that follow, you will find appropriate remedies and crystals to support your psychic intention. You will also find case histories from several practitioners to show you what has worked in actual situations.

Using Visualization

There are guided visualization exercises throughout this book. Using imagery is easy, once you know how. Visualization employs 'mind pictures' to bring things into being. It is creating with your mind, your will and your intent. To promote these pictures, you can close your eyes and look up to a place above and between your eyebrows, making an 'inner screen'. However, many people, even with their eyes closed, 'see' things about two feet in front of them, as though the images are being projected forward. Some people 'see' the picture from within as though it is happening all around them. Other people will never 'see' anything at all but will get a strong sense or feel of what is happening.

You need to practise to find out exactly how you will 'see'. You may find that nothing seems to be happening, in which case you have to 'act as if'. Acting as if means that you have trust in the inner process. That you mentally go through the exercises, remembering that the power of thought is the most powerful creator there is. You use the force of your will and your intention, focussing your energy on the exercise and believing that, on some level, it is happening. (Several of the exercises have hand or body movements to help in this process.)

When doing the exercises, create a safe space in which to work (see page 55). It is important to choose a time when you will not be disturbed. With all of the exercises, stopping in the middle leaves you vulnerable. Begin by reading the exercise through. You may like to tape it, with appropriate pauses, or have a friend read it to you but if you are doing it from memory, read the exercise several times before attempting it.

Relaxation is a key to visualization. You cannot visualize if you are tense or nervous. Choose a place where there is little outside disturbance and sit or lie in a comfortable position. Spend a few moments breathing quietly, withdrawing your thoughts from the outside world and centring your attention deep within your self. Allow your body and your mind to quieten. (If you need extra help with relaxation, see page 101). Then, when you are ready, close your eyes and begin the exercise. Go at the pace which is right for you, taking as long as you need. Straining to make the images come is counter-productive, it only makes it harder. Sometimes your mind will throw up a picture which is somewhat different from the exercise in the book. If this happens consider the image. Is it helpful? Is it appropriate for you? If so, then use this image adapting the wording in the exercise appropriately.

Closing down afterwards is also important. All the exercises finish with a closing and grounding section. Do not skip this. When you have finished, get up and move around, have a good stretch. Have a cup of tea. Do something practical. All of this helps you to be grounded again.

Practise the exercise until it becomes automatic. You only have to think 'light bubble' for instance, and your aura is protected and surrounded by light. Then, when you need it, it will be an instinctive process.

Using Flower Essences and Crystals

Flower Essences (available from the stockists listed in the Appendix) are usually supplied in a 'stock' formula, with the exception of some of the purpose-made Protection Essences. To prepare a stock formula for use, put one-third brandy and two-thirds spring water into a dropper bottle and add seven drops of the stock formula. Take 1–7 drops three times a day, or more often in acute cases.

Essences can be evaporated into your aura by placing a few drops in the palms of your hands and running your hands around your body without touching it. They can also be applied to the chakras. Essences can be put into your bath water or sprayed around the room. To spray, put spring water into a clean spray bottle or mister and add seven drops of the essence together with a few drops of essential oils such as lavender or Geranium if appropriate. Some essences can also be used on an oil burner or dropped onto a crystal or light bulb.

Chakra

Energy centre that links the physical and energetic bodies.

Crystals are particularly effective for psychic protection and have been used for thousands of years for this purpose. Scientists have shown that black crystals actually absorb energy. (Crystals in other colours absorb energy and put it out again in exactly the same amount, although it may have been transformed or transmuted in the process.) The fact that black crystals work differently suggests that they are dumping the absorbed energy into the 'dustbin dimension', a subtle realm which can absorb negative energy and render it harmless. This may well be why black crystals such as **black tourmaline** or **smoky quartz** are particularly effective in cases of psychic attack, and why an **Apache Tear** (translucent **black obsidian**) absorbs negative energy released during therapy or healing work.

The Dustbin Dimension

An area of space, inner or outer, that is vibrating at a rate that 'swallows up' negative energy and transmutes it into positive energy.

Before using a crystal it should be cleansed. Spraying with **Crystal Clear** (Petal) is an excellent way to cleanse any crystal. Crystals can also be cleansed by soaking in water and salt and then placing in sunlight to dry.

When using a crystal for protection, most are worn around the neck (either as purpose made jewellery or in a wire spiral). Crystals can also be placed on the body or within a room. To 'programme' a crystal, hold it in your hands for a few moments, focus your attention on the crystal, and ask that it will work for you in the best way possible to protect and cleanse you and your space, to protect your energies, etc.

Flower Essence Manufacturer Abbreviations Used in this Book:

Aid	Second Aid
Al	Alaskan
Arare	Araretama
Aloha	Aloha Flower Essences
Bach	Bach Flower Essences
Bailey	The Bailey Flower Essences
Bush	Australian Bush Flower Essences
Fes	Flower Essence Services
Hare	Harebell
Him	Aum Himalayan Flower Essences
Korte	(Korte PHI Essenz)
Pa	Pacific Flower Essences
Petal	Petaltone Essences
SA	South African F.E.
West	Western Australian Essences

ONE

THE HISTORY OF Psychic Protection

Psychic protection has been practised for thousands of years. The ancient dead were buried with amulets and tokens to aid their journey to another world. The living wore talismans and crystals, chanted spells and incantations. For 'primitive man' the boundaries between the worlds was diffuse. Spirits could, and did, interfere in the lives of men. These were not just spirits who had departed from the everyday world of the living. There was an abode of demons and djinns, evil spirits whose delight was to adversely affect day-to-day events. So, for early man, the psychic world was a very real, and potentially dangerous, place. To counteract this, priests and priestesses studied magic and wielded great power.

Much of the religion was directed to controlling the powers and denizens of darkness by attracting benevolent beings. The Egyptians wanted to command their gods, to set them actively to work on their behalf. They also wanted to ensure that the dead stayed where they were supposed to be: in the tomb and *Amenti*, the Other World. All but the poorest of Egyptians routinely wore a protective amulet or magical charm. The Eye of Horus, or the Buckle of Isis, warded off the 'evil eye' and guaranteed protection.

The Egyptians were known as a nation of sorcerers and magicians: experts in occult arts. Controlling spirits and magical forces was a science. Six thousand years ago, Egyptian knowledge of both the afterlife and of manipulating magical forces was set down on papyri and in hieroglyphs – themselves magical symbols. Some of this knowledge may seem like mere superstition, but there is an enormous amount of wisdom to be found there. We can still use the same talismans and precious stones today. Their perception of the subtle bodies has much to teach us. The Egyptians recognized not only the physical body but also the shadow, the soul, the spirit and the *ka* or etheric body which was the vehicle for astral travel and beyond-death continuity of consciousness.

Protective amulets: Eye of Horus and Buckle of Isis

Astral Travel

The ability of part of our consciousness to leave the physical body and journey on its own to other realms.

It is not only in Egyptian literature that the fame of the Egyptian magicians lingers. Nor were the Egyptians the only ones skilled in magic. The plagues of Egypt were brought down upon an unsuspecting population by a Hebrew magician. The biblical story of Moses and Aaron graphically portrays the world of magic – and illustrates how psychic attack works no matter what the culture:

> *Aaron threw down his staff in front of Pharaoh and his courtiers, and it turned into a serpent. At this, Pharaoh summoned the wise men and the sorcerers, and the Egyptian magicians too did the same thing by their spells. Every man threw his staff down, and each staff turned into a serpent, but Aaron's staff swallowed up theirs ... So Moses and Aaron did as the Lord had commanded. He [sic] lifted up his staff and struck the water of the Nile ... and all the water was changed into blood. The fish died and the river stank ... Aaron stretched out his hand over the waters of Egypt, and the frogs came up and covered the land ... Aaron stretched out his staff and struck the dust, and it turned into maggots on man and beast ... swarms of flies ... all the herds of Egypt died ... festering boils [affected] men and beasts [but only the Egyptians, the Israelites were unharmed] ... violent hailstorms ... thunder and fire ... locusts ... darkness over the land of Egypt ... and [finally] every firstborn son of Egypt died. (Exodus 4–12)*

All this, if the bible is to be believed, so that Pharaoh would be forced to let the Israelites leave Egypt.

There are no extant accounts of this great magical battle in Egyptian literature, but there are plenty of accounts of other battles. A papyrus in the British Museum tells the story of Siusire, son of Setna:

An Ethiopian magician came to Egypt, a sealed letter in his hand. He challenged the Egyptian magicians to read the letter without opening it. No one could and so Egypt was humiliated by Ethiopia. This, Setna tells his son, is why he, Setna, suffers from depression. Siusire tells his father not to worry, he knows how to read the letter.

Meanwhile, the Ethiopian magician has fashioned a litter and four porters in wax and used it to magically transport Pharaoh, in the form of his *ka*, to Ethiopia. He is given five hundred strokes of a cane and returned to Egypt. His court magician tries to prevent a repeat performance, calling on Thoth, the great god who invented magic, to protect the Pharaoh. Thoth appears to the magician in a dream, telling him to go to the temple of Khnum where he will find a papyrus. He is to take a copy and make protective amulets so that Pharaoh cannot be carried off again. The Egyptian magicians in turn make a litter to carry the king of Ethiopia to the Egyptian court, where he is given five hundred strokes of the cane. When the king awakes, he is bruised and he concludes that he has fallen under an evil spell. Twice more the king is recalled to Egypt and punished.

Finally, the Egyptian and Ethiopian magicians meet face to face in a great magical battle – a battle which is a repeat of one which took place 1500 years earlier. Siusire is the link between the two events. He was present at both and then, as now, defeats the Ethiopian magician.

The Egyptians believed in reincarnation, especially when it had fate or destiny behind it. Siusire's destiny was to defeat his former adversaries in his new life.

Amulets, which guaranteed 'vital function', and protective charms are important in Egyptian magic. They were made from precious stones, gold, glass, bronze and faience. The heart scarab, a symbol of metamorphosis and change, was buried with the dead (one of 104 such amulets). Placing a scarab on the heart of a mummy conferred power to overcome fierce attacks in the other world. Prepared whilst its owner was still alive, its purpose was to make the heart 'of heavenly origin' so that it beat with, and awoke perception of, the invisible and thus conferred immunity to psychic attack both before and after death.

The *Leyden Magical Papyrus* gives a 'recipe' for preparing a protective talisman from linen with sixteen threads (four each of white, green, blue and red), which is then died with the blood of a hoopoe bird and tied to a scarab in the form of the sun god robed in finest linen. Such amulets and talismans usually featured the gods, sacred animals and a representation of the Pharaoh that conferred powers and attributes associated with Pharaoh. Words were then pronounced over the amulet to imbue it with power – in effect blessing it against the powers of evil.

Ancient Egyptians were both aware of, and afraid of, the power of deceased souls to reach back to touch the living. There was no 'insuperable barrier' between the two realms. The souls of the dead could be both malevolent and benevolent in intention. Letters were written by the living to the dead, usually inscribed on bowls or pieces of papyrus. The letters sometimes asked for intervention and assistance with problems. At other times, as in a famous letter, they were pleas to be left in peace.

A couple had been happily married before the wife died – lingeringly from an incurable disease. The husband went into deep mourning. He scarcely ate or drank, and cried without ceasing at her tomb. Three years later he was still in deep sorrow. He felt bewitched. In a letter to his wife he wrote:

> *What evil have you wrought to bring me to this painful state in which I find myself? What have I done to justify your laying hands on me, when I have committed no unkindness against you? ... I accuse you through these words, before the Ennead [gods] who are in the West, and judgement will be passed on you and upon the letter which contains the facts of this affair. What have I done that you should act thus?*
>
> (QUOTED IN MAGIC AND MYSTERY IN ANCIENT EGYPT, CHRISTIAN JACQ, SOUVENIR PRESS, 1998, PAGE 72)

Nowadays, he would probably be diagnosed by a metaphysician as suffering from a particularly nasty case of psychic attachment or emotional overwhelm.

Egyptian ideas passed down through the Greeks, Romans, Arabs and reached as far as India and the British Isles. It is possible they reached South America. We can still find many Egyptian ideas in esoteric teachings and mystery schools which claim direct descent from this ancient civilization, and in Christianity today. (The Mary to whom Catholics pray for protection is a metamorphosis of Isis, the Divine Mother, to whom the Egyptians prayed for over three thousand years.)

Emotional Overwhelm

Emotional overwhelm occurs when someone else's emotions take over to such an extent that it is impossible to separate them out from one's own. It can also be a totally overwhelming emotion such as grief taking over to the exclusion of all else.

In the West during the Middle Ages, there was a roaring trade in amulets. Bones of the saints, pieces of 'the True Cross' and other relics were said to assure the faithful of divine protection. People still sought the help of 'the Old Religion' for talismans and spells. As time went on, the Buckle of Isis had changed into a crucifix or holy medal but its purpose was still the same.

With the rise of occultism in the nineteenth and twentieth centuries, many of the ancient practices were revived and the protective function aroused to guard initiates who travelled between the worlds. Initiation was a prerequisite to magical working. Much studying was called for. To a great extent, the initiates were protected by their carefully acquired knowledge – although some went adventuring where it was not wise for the unwary to tread. And, of course, there were the pioneers who 'plucked out of the ether' a supposed memory of how it had been. By the end of the twentieth century, occult knowledge was freely available to all – much of it abused or misunderstood, leaving practitioners wide open to psychic invasion of all kinds.

TWO

WHAT IS Psychic Protection

You may think you know what protection means – and assume that you are well protected. At a national level, the armed forces 'defend the realm', the police 'keep us safe'. At a personal level you wear wellington boots and a waterproof coat to repel the rain. You may keep a dog to watch over you while you sleep. You no doubt insure the house and the car in case of theft or accident. You can install alarms against fire or intruders. 'Protection' is an industry worth millions of pounds.

But have you ever stopped to think that there is something else against which you may need to defend yourself? An intrusion which is silent, invisible, and yet very powerful. An unseen force that operates not in the physical world, but in the psychic realm: an environment which requires a special kind of protection. People's thoughts and feelings are intense and, unless you have a strong aura and take steps to protect yourself when in difficult circumstances, it is easy to pick up unwanted vibes. You may also be unwittingly 'attacking yourself' through negative thought patterns and destructive emotional states. This is where psychic protection comes in.

At its simplest level, psychic protection is anything that strengthens your aura and creates a safe space. Such protection can be visualized as a light bubble you inhabit, or a shiny new dustbin into which you mentally jump and pull down the lid. Protection can be physicallized as a crystal you wear, a talisman you keep at your side. The Star of David, for instance, is an ancient talisman for protection. If you work with other people (or have a stressed-out visitor to your home), then gentle rituals like lighting a candle or incense, spraying with flower essences or burning essential oils, or placing a bowl of water in the room can help. So too can creating a safe space in which to work – a ritual that need take less than five minutes of your time but which will be invaluable in its results.

Safe Space

A place, large or small, which is protected and cleansed so that nothing untoward can penetrate or interfere with what goes on in that space.

Rituals work not because of some inherent magical powers, but because they focus your attention. It is will, and intention, that provide the strongest protection. You can make a ritual out of spraying the room – and yourself – with a special space-clearing essence when your client or visitor leaves. This ensures that nothing adverse is left behind, that all the emotions or negative energies are safely dispersed. (Space clearing also makes your living quarters much nicer on a day-to-day level – it takes out any emotional and mental stress or discord and aids well-being, which in turn protects.)

Simple, instinctive acts can give you psychic protection. Many people find themselves crossing their arms over their solar plexus when the atmosphere around them becomes too emotionally charged. The solar plexus is one of the places where your body feels invaded by other people's strong emotions, and where they can drain your energy – your belly is another. Some people are sensitive to other people's thoughts too. Most of us at some time or another have had the experience of having a thought pop into our head that isn't *our own*. But, there are people who are constantly bombarded by other people's stray thoughts. When it all gets too much, you will see people instinctively putting their hands over their ears, trying to blot out the invasion. But, as the intrusion is psychic not physical, this is rarely sufficient. Psychic protection screens off the thoughts and feelings that invade your space. It creates a safe space in which to relax, to meditate, or simply to be in the world without fear of invasion by something or someone outside yourself.

However, not all psychic encroachment comes from outside yourself. Your own negative thoughts and feelings, especially those you suppress, may well be causing you psychic unease, and could well attract to you exactly what you most fear. Psychic protection also entails knowing yourself, having an inner spring clean to let go of the destructive patterns that lurk unsuspected deep within yourself.

THREE

WHY IS PSYCHIC Protection Required?

Psychic protection is needed because, for reasons which will become clear, certain people are open to intrusion at a subtle, energetic level. There are people whose boundaries are diffuse, whose energy leaks out and who have nothing to stop someone else's energy going *in*. These people may have taken up meditation, self-hypnosis, healing, counselling. They have learned to open up their intuition and make contact with different levels of consciousness, but may not be aware of the need to close down again afterwards. They may have damaged their aura in some way. A 'holey' aura allows two-way traffic of energy: out and in. Some people are born with a 'leaky aura'. You may well be one of these people.

Leaky Aura

A 'leaky aura' means there are gaps in the subtle energy field that surrounds and protects the physical body. A 'leaky aura' looks rather like a sieve and allows emotions, energy or mental influences to pass into, or be drawn out of, a person's psychic space without that person being aware of the process, or its effects.

Do You Need Psychic Protection?

Many people instinctively know when they are in need of psychic protection. They feel *wrong*, uneasy or invaded. But you may be unsure as to whether you need to protect yourself or not. The following list will help you to identify a potential need:

- Do you work closely with other people?
- Do you use recreational drugs?
- Do people bring you their troubles?
- Do you give a great deal of energy to other people?
- Do certain people or places leave you feeling drained and tired?
- Are you sensitive to atmospheres?
- Are you ungrounded, 'head in the clouds'?
- Do you cry easily?
- Do you feel low if a friend is depressed or unhappy?
- Do you feel disturbed if a friend is angry?
- Do you use relaxation tapes? Meditate? Journey? Do you do yoga or tai chi chuan?
- Are you accident prone?
- Have many small things gone wrong recently?
- Do you lose things?
- Do you suffer from nightmares and poor sleep?
- Are you anxious, nervy, on edge all the time?
- Do you have invisible feelers out, testing the air around you?
- Are you afraid to relax?
- Are you perpetually tired, listless, hopeless?
- Do you find yourself glancing over your shoulder because you sense you are being watched, only to discover there is no one there?
- Do you suffer from a sense of dis-ease, feeling ill but not in a physical way?
- Have you ever felt invaded, somehow *not yourself*?
- Do you dwell on things, turning them over and over in your mind?
- Has anyone shown particularly strong animosity to you?

- Do you feel someone 'has it in for you'?
- Do you have more enemies than friends?
- Were you born under the sign of Cancer, Scorpio or Pisces?
- Do you believe you are psychic – do you have 'hunches'?
- Have you ever seen a ghost?
- Did you have a particularly authoritarian childhood?
- Do you find it hard to say no?

If you answer yes to more than two of the above, then the chances are you need psychic protection. You may well be one of those people who are naturally vulnerable to psychic intrusion.

The Astrological Element

Astrologically speaking, the water element is the psychic element and people who have a strong water emphasis in their horoscope are sensitive to psychic energy. So, if you were born under a water sign (Cancer, Scorpio or Pisces), or have one of these signs as your Ascendant, or the planet Neptune close to your Ascendant; or if your Moon is in a water sign, then you are potentially more vulnerable at a subtle, psychic level. Likewise if you have strong Neptune aspects to your Sun, Moon or Mercury. Consulting an astrologer will aid you in identifying if you are at risk in this way.

The Emotional Element

Strong emotions can also precipitate a need for psychic defences. When people are tired, depressed, tearful, angry or fearful, they are more vulnerable to psychic vampirism or attack. During periods of deep grief, there can be danger of psychic attachment – holding onto or being held onto by the person who has died or left. Equally, people in the grip of strong emotion are more likely themselves to attack psychically – often without knowing what they are doing.

Acupuncture can aid healing in cases where emotional overwhelm has weakened the psychic energy. The following case study shows how important timing can be in dealing with chronic conditions and how persisting with a treatment may be necessary before relief is found:

CASE HISTORY: LOOKING LIFE IN THE EYE

Having seen his father die slowly and painfully when he was a teenager, but having never properly grieved for his father as he was away at boarding school when the death occurred, a man reached the age of 50 still carrying the weight of that grief. He looked 'haunted'. He was unable to look anyone in the eye and suffered from a disorganized, chaotic life. He worked with patients and was prone to 'losing energy'. Regular practice of Tai Chi Chuan and Qi Gong kept his energy up, but there were times when his energy crashed, especially when he was dealing with patients who had strong emotional needs. His acupuncturist had given him several treatments to release 'possession by strong emotions' but none had been entirely successful.

When his mother died, he feared that he would be 'too tired to deal with clearing out her house'. He found it difficult to express his grief – being used to bottling everything up. In extreme emotional overload, he had one further treatment for 'possession'. By the next day his eyes were clear, he looked people in the eye and he had the energy not only to clear out his mother's house but also to reorganize his own home and working space.

Flower Essences for Emotional Overwhelm
Sturt Desert Pea – grief; Bottlebrush (Bush).

The Physical Element

The physical state of your body, its internal balance or imbalance, can affect your need for psychic protection. The body has subtle physiological processes that affect mood and psychic openness. Hormones, enzymes and endorphins all play their part in regulating psychic experience. Adolescence and menopause, when hormones are most out of balance, are often times of great psychic receptivity and emotional overwhelm. Balancing out the body can create powerful protection, as can monitoring the foods that you put into your body.

Blood sugar imbalances can be responsible for mood swings and uncontrolled psychic invasion. If your body is addicted to sugar (and sugar forms a high percentage of alcohol, sweets and cakes), then it can lead to a serotonin–endorphin imbalance. One of the symptoms of beta-endorphin deficiency is being overwhelmed by others' pain. The symptoms of low blood sugar bear a striking resemblance to those of psychic vulnerability: constant tiredness, confusion, frustration, irritability and memory loss. By regulating the amount of sugar

you take in, and controlling your blood-sugar with meals that contain high levels of complex starches (green vegetables and 'brown' products such as rice and flour), you can maintain your physiological processes at the optimum level for the best natural psychic protection.

Activities to Increase Endorphins
Meditation, Jogging and Exercise, Acupuncture, Sex.

Increasing Serotonin Levels
Negative ions or ioniser, Melatonin (not legal in England), Bananas (but they also put up blood sugar).

Flower Essence for Balancing Blood Sugar
Peach Flowered Tea Tree (Bush).

Other substances taken into the body can also affect its psychic defences. Few drug addicts realize that their habit can actually destroy a natural protection against psychic invasion. It is as though the crown chakras and the natural 'gates' in the brain that usually protect, have been blown wide open. A 'bad trip' is often the result of sensitivity to negative energies – energies which may come from the psyche, from the people around or from other levels of being. But you don't need to be an addict to experience a temporary cessation of natural protection. A few shots of alcohol too many (alcohol is a drug) and it is not only your inhibitions that you lose. You can be subtly affected by unseen energies – and entities. Prescribed medication (especially tranquillizers and anti-depressants) can have the same effect, as can certain herbs (the Aloha flower essence **Paini-Awa'Awa** can heal damage from psychotropic drugs).

Having poor body awareness can also affect your psychic defences. If you are unaware of how much physical space you take up, then you are unlikely to accurately define 'your space'. You may find it difficult to untangle your energies from those of another person. There are people who always intrude onto the space of someone else when trying to communicate – the 'in your face' stance where someone stands much too close. This can arise from inadequate boundaries and literally not knowing where 'me' ends and 'you' begin. (It may also be a deliberate ploy as intimidation, physical or psychic, may have been found to be effective in getting what that person wants.)

If you feel that you may have impaired body awareness, then getting a friend to draw around your outline onto a large piece of paper can help. As can looking in a mirror and tracing your outline with your fingers. You can also ask a friend to help you establish where your boundaries are. Get them to walk towards you, and ask them to stop when it feels uncomfortable for you. Then ask them to walk back until you feel comfortable again. This will show you 'your space', the area you need around yourself in order to feel safe and protected. Body or breath work, yoga, tai chi and similar activities can help you to become more aware of your body and to be fully grounded within it.

Damage to or scarring of the physical body can also affect your ability to hold your energy together and prevent psychic leakage.

CASE HISTORY: ABDOMINAL SCARRING

A woman was aware of a sense of weakness in her abdomen. She felt she lost energy in that part of her body and was constantly depleted, especially from contact with needy people and during sexual contact. Some years previously she had undergone a sterilization operation which had penetrated the wall of her abdomen below her navel and above her pubic bone. At these points, physical scars were visible. Seen clairvoyantly, her energy at these two sites was grey and ragged. The energy flow around her body, and her aura, was blocked, leaving the area weak and vulnerable. Energy could 'leak' out at these points. A magnet was used to 'knit' the broken energy together and return the aura to its normal magnetic vibration. This was followed up with the Australian Bush Flower Essence Slender Rice Flower which heals physical scarring. Her abdominal energy was restored.

Symptoms of Psychic Vulnerability

Another way of identifying a need to safeguard or cleanse your energies is to look at how you feel, and what you experience, on a day-to-day basis. (Keeping a journal can be useful.) Spend a few moments reviewing your average day and monitoring your energy levels. Notice especially if you suffer from any of the following:

- Overwhelming demands made by other people
- No sense of space for yourself
- Extremes of emotion
- Lethargy and listlessness
- Chronic fatigue
- Depression
- ME and other chronic illnesses
- Feeling of helplessness
- Unexplained rage
- Dependence on others
- Insomnia

- Irrationality
- Mind will not switch off
- Schizophrenia and psychotic states
- Sense of being watched or communicated with by someone other
- Domination by another person
- Inability to concentrate
- Ungroundedness
- Head in the clouds
- Lacking in boundaries
- Overly sympathetic
- Overly concerned for others
- Feeling guilty

All of the above are signs that you may well be vulnerable at a psychic level. Vulnerability at this level can lead to psychic invasion – that is, being open to your subtle energies being penetrated by those of someone else. Psychic invasion can in turn lead to other conditions detrimental to your psychic health such as vampirism and attachment.

Psychic Invasion

Being open to penetration on a subtle level by the energies of someone else.

How Psychic Invasion Can Occur

Psychic invasion occurs through a weak aura. The aura becomes weak when it is neglected, when it has been attacked, or has become impaired by illness or emotional stress. Some people are born with a strong aura, and manage to maintain that strength no matter what. Other people are born with a much less robust aura. Still other people find their aura has been damaged by an operation or by the actions of another person.

Auras are particularly vulnerable in childhood. If a child is seen as an extension of a parent, with no personal autonomy, then the child's aura can be 'swallowed up' by the parent. The child is engulfed within the parental aura. The relationship is symbiotic and energy will pass freely between child and parent – many parents unknowingly 'vampirize' their child's energy to strengthen their own. Similarly, if a child is taught to see him- or herself as weak and powerless, then the aura suffers. Unless things change drastically, such views of oneself are carried beyond childhood and subtly affect the adult aura.

Auras can meld in both passion and anger. Just as in childhood a parent's aura can engulf, so too can a lover's. Those who can see the aura describe it 'surging and moving' towards the object of one's affections – or of one's displeasure. The colours merge and mingle. It is an old esoteric teaching that you should be careful who you sleep with. Old lovers can leave their imprint in your aura, but so too can someone with whom there is a more casual contact.

Psychic Penetration

When your aura is 'weak', it appears rather like a lace curtain. The edges are ragged, diffuse. The colours are pale and patchy. Seen clairvoyantly, psychic invasion is like a hook going in through a hole. If a predatory female comes across a male whose aura is weak, she may well project her sexual allure. But at the same time, her aura will surge forward and rush into a convenient breach – clairvoyantly seen as a 'hook'.

If this hooking in is at the level of the solar plexus, seat of the emotions, then he may well respond with, seeming, 'love'. At the level of the lower chakras, lust is the response. At a mental level, she is his 'ideal woman'. Whichever way, she, literally, has him hooked. He may feel he has met his soulmate, his one true love. He may persist in this delusion for quite sometime. But, when disillusionment eventually sets in, he will find it hard to disentangle himself. He will undoubtedly suffer from low energy, especially if she has been feeding her self-esteem off his emotional energy.

The 'rejection' will be experienced strongly by his erstwhile partner, who will fight to reel him in again. If he does not completely cut the ties with her, then she will maintain that link into his emotional energy long after the relationship has ceased. If the original breach was through the heart centre, it will be his heart energy which will be weakened. In such a case, he is likely to maintain the delusion that this is his soulmate. If she leaves him, he could, quite literally, die of a 'broken heart' and will certainly *feel* as though this is happening. Tie cutting aids the clearing, see page 54.

However, any relationship, when it breaks up, can create a feeling of psychic invasion as this story from David Lawson demonstrates:

CASE HISTORY: JULIA'S STORY

Julia was an attractive woman in her mid-thirties who visited me for spiritual healing and some guidance about a failed marriage that had left her feeling drained. Her ex-husband, while appearing keen to move on from their relationship, was focusing a great deal of anger and sexual need in her direction. Julia would go to bed at night and do her best to settle down to sleep. Within an hour or so she would be fully conscious and fearful. She had the feeling that her ex-husband was in her bedroom, watching her, goading her and angrily wishing to 'possess' her sexually. While she didn't feel touched in the physical sense, she did have the feeling that a woman has when a man undresses her with his eyes and has abusive fantasies about her.

At first she thought she was going crazy and put her experiences down to her own separation anxieties but as this invasion continued to occur, she came to realize that this was not of her own making. When Julia visited me she was tired, scared and aware that her confidence was ebbing away on a nightly basis.

After using some hands-on healing techniques to balance and recharge Julia's vital energy, I gently began to disperse some energetic attachments from her auric field. In further sessions I made the process a more conscious one and guided Julia through some cord-cutting exercises so that she herself could take control of the situation. We also put together an action plan of practical steps she could take at home. As Julia's bedroom and bed were once shared by them both, I suggested she clear from the room anything she associated with her husband, bought new bed linen and gave the whole house a spring clean.

At the end of each session I helped Julia to build a cocoon of psychic protection around herself and develop a subtle magnetism to positive influences. I also advised her to assert herself whenever she felt invaded by her husband. The way Julia chose to do this was by sitting up in bed, turning on the light and firmly asking her husband to leave.

David commented that it is rarely valuable to apportion blame in a situation like this. Julia's husband may have been totally unconscious of what he was doing. Indeed, he may even have been asleep at the time. Blame can keep people attached to their problems rather than release them. Making ourselves less available for psychic attack and more available for positive influences is a much more effective use of our time and energy. With Julia, it was important for her to exercise forgiveness at the same time as strengthening her psychic boundaries. This combined approach proved highly effective in clearing her psychic invasion and in revealing some underlying issues that had been present since childhood. Many adults have emotional or mental energy attached to them that is left over from the problems and disturbances of childhood and these attachments may attract further psychic invasion throughout life. Unexpressed or unconscious feelings may be felt as the child's own and can create an availability for later psychic interference whether consciously or unconsciously directed from other people or non-physical entities.

David went on to say that Julia's healing process was a little like peeling off the layers of an onion. Each step she took to resolve the situation with her husband uncovered a level of psychic invasion that had come from Julia's father. She came to realize that she had always felt invaded by her father's unconscious anger and sexual frustration and that this childhood psychic disturbance had created an availability for unhealthy patterns in her adult relationships. After

just a short time, Julia was free of her husband's psychic interference and after a few months she felt like a totally new woman. Julia became energized and confident, secure in her own home and better able to form new relationships.

FOUR

THE Aura

To clairvoyants (those with the gift of psychic sight), the aura is a weaving, intermingling field of coloured lights shooting out from the body, sometimes to a width of six feet or so depending on conditions. For those without the gift of psychic sight, the aura can sometimes be glimpsed as a whitish or coloured glow around the head, especially when seen against a neutral background.

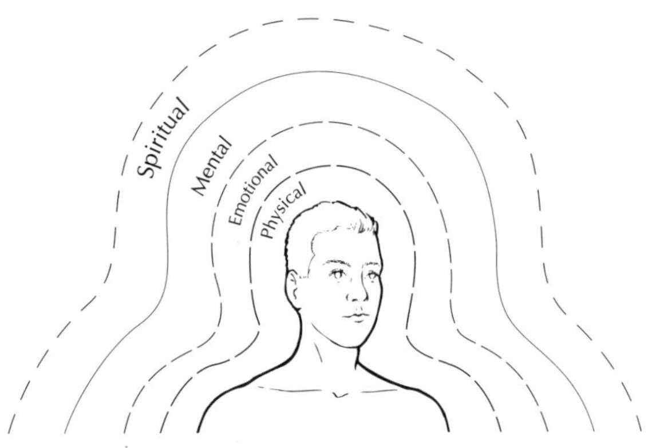

The aura is often known as the 'energy body' because of its vital and energetic appearance. It has a characteristic energy field, which can be seen, felt or measured in various ways. This energy can, for instance, be photographed with a kirlian camera.

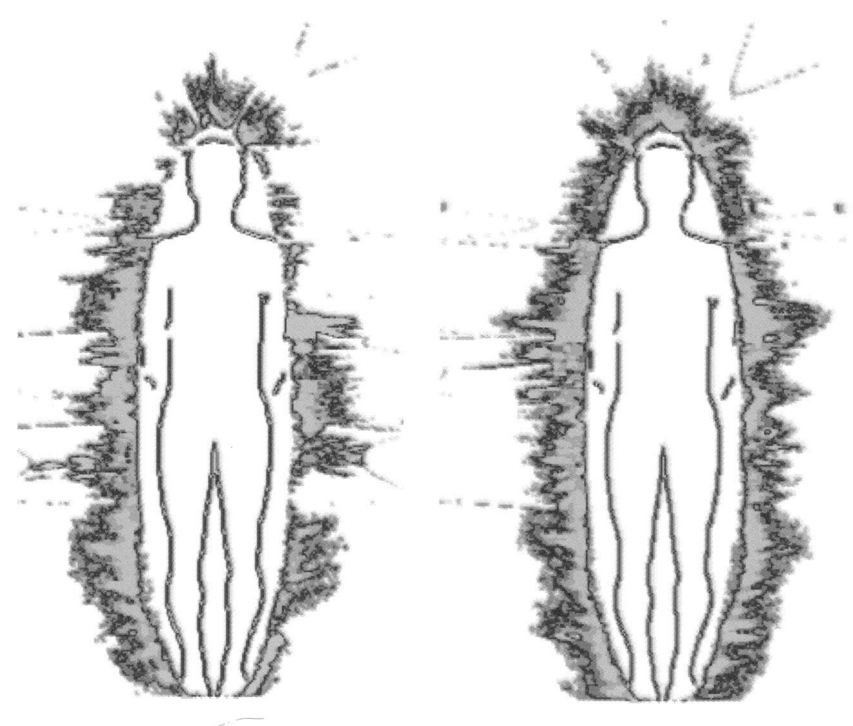

The aura captured by a kirlian camera: a) An unprotected aura b) Energy protected by a flower essence

The first illustration shows an unprotected aura. The second shows the aura when a psychic protection essence is held in the hand. A clear difference is visible, a difference that will be maintained whether the remedy is passed through the energy field or taken internally. From the second picture, it can be seen that the area around the throat is still a little weak. Additional protection could be used here, such as wearing a **turquoise** crystal, or taking **Authenticity** (Him) flower essence to strengthen the throat chakra.

The Etheric Body

The physical body is not our only body. We also have subtle bodies on the emotional, mental and spiritual levels, each vibrating at a different rate or frequency. Each of these bodies has an aura and the whole is housed within the 'etheric body' (the ancient Egyptian *ka*).

> ## Etheric Body (Ka)
>
> *The subtle body that houses the emotional, mental and spiritual bodies and forms a vehicle for the soul to move around independently of the physical body.*

The Composition of the Aura

The aura consists of coloured 'bands'. Different layers and levels relate to different functions. Closest to the physical level and to your body, the aura reveals your state of health: your 'ease' or dis'ease'. Move out a bit and you are into the emotional aura. The mental aura shows your intellectual and mental activity, and the outer spiritual aura is your link to the more subtle levels of being (see illustration page 30 and in chapter 5, pages 45 and 50).

Auric Protection

As we have seen, the state of your aura determines how well protected you are on a personal level. Many people have no idea how far their aura extends, or whether it is strong or weak. Your aura is like a mirror. It reflects how you are. When you have intense emotions and feelings, your aura tends to expand out from the solar plexus. Anger produces a vivid red colour, jealousy is often green, whilst compassion may well show itself as blue. If you have been doing strong intellectual work, then it is probable that the aura around your head has expanded considerably. It is likely to be yellow in colour. If the work was left-brained – concerned with analysis and reason – then the aura may well jut out to the left. If on the other hand, you have been using your intuitive and imaginative right-brain, then the aura could billow out to the right.

If you have been thinking about someone, then a piece of your aura may have formed into a 'tentacle' which has reached out toward them. In extreme situations, it may even have attached to them, and could separate and remain attached to them rather than staying with your own aura. This is like giving away a piece of yourself to someone else (a similar situation can occur with your heart when an intense love affair ends).

Seeing the Aura

It is possible to train yourself to see how far your aura extends. Standing against a white or pale coloured background and looking into a mirror with the lights dimmed will often enable you to glimpse your aura, especially if you choose a time when you have been working on an intuitive or intellectual level. This works best if you do not stare straight at the mirror but rather look off to the side somewhat. At first, you tend to catch a glimpse out of the corner of your eye which fades when you try to focus on it. It improves with practise. However, you can also train yourself to *feel* your aura or to *sense* it.

Exercise: Feeling the Aura

Choosing a time when you are calm and relaxed and unlikely to be disturbed, stand so that you can reach out around yourself. (The exercise can be performed sitting if you prefer and with your eyes open or closed, whichever feels more appropriate).

Spend a few moments breathing quietly and easily and attuning to your body.

Then take your attention down to the palms of the hands. As you focus your attention you may find that your palms begin to tingle.

Reach up above your head and use your hands to sense where your aura is. You will probably be aware of it as an energy field. Check how far out it extends. Move your hands around the edges of your aura from your head to your feet. Begin in front of your body and go from above the head down to your feet. Then do the sides and finally the back of your body. (If you cannot reach with your hands use your mind to check out this area). Check how far out the aura extends and notice any places where the energy breaks up or feels different in any way.

If you find that your aura extends a long way out, or is close to your body, try playing with the aura. Use your hand to pull or push it into a more appropriate distance from your body.

Then go over your entire aura checking for breaks and 'holes' (which can feel 'cold' or energy-less). Use your hands to put extra energy into that place, pulling the edges of the aura together. (You may notice that something is attached to your aura. If you do and it is possible to remove it, do so and then picture a plaster of healing light sealing up the place where it was attached.)

Then experiment with your aura and the ability your mind has to control it. If your eyes are open, close them gently. Picture your aura expanding, and then contracting. Really let yourself feel the process happening. (If necessary check with your hands that the aura has responded). Push it in, and draw it out until you feel comfortable with the process. Then let your aura settle at an appropriate distance from your body.

When you are ready, open your eyes. Take your attention down to your feet and feel your feet on the earth. Be aware that your feet are connected to the earth, grounding you. With your eyes wide open, take a deep breath and stand up with your feet firmly on the earth.

(If you find it difficult to visualize, use your hands to sense where your aura is and continue until you can sense where it is with your mind alone.)

This exercise should be performed once or twice a day until you can instinctively feel where your aura is at any time simply by closing your eyes for a moment and scanning your body. In this way, you will become aware if your energy starts to drain out or if something tries to invade your aura. Whenever you have to enter a crowd of people, you will find it beneficial to encase your aura in a light bubble for protection, but you may well find that certain people invoke a desire to safeguard your energy in this way. Once you have identified who brings up this response, you can summon up your light bubble before you need it.

Exercise: The Light Bubble

Using the power of your mind, picture your aura entirely surrounded and enclosed by light. (You may find it easiest to start with a light over your head and bring this down around your body, working towards your feet). Make sure that the light bubble goes under your feet and seals itself there.

(You can also 'crystallize' the outer edges of your aura for additional protection. Simply visualize yourself standing inside a large, hollow, crystal that is filled with light.)

Checking the Aura with a Crystal

You can also use a crystal to check your aura. Holding it in your hand, gently move it around your body whilst attuning to the energies. A quartz crystal will help you to detect 'holes', amber cleans the aura, and labradorite heals it. If you find anything attached to your aura, then a selenite crystal can help to detach it.

The Aura and Spiritual Healing

Spiritual healing is an excellent method of repairing the aura and realigning the different energy bodies. In the hands of a skilled healer, negative energies can be drawn out, 'holes' healed and disharmonies eliminated. In the hands of an inexperienced, or unwise, healer these symptoms can be created. If you feel worse rather than better after spiritual, or any other form of healing, it is as well to check that the healer is not, intentionally or otherwise, draining your energy.

Acupuncture, shiatsu and other body-based therapies can also help to realign auric imbalances.

Flower Essences for the Aura

Angelsword (Bush) – raises vibrations; Araryba (Arare) – reconstructs; Auric Protection (Aid, SA and FES); Aura Cleaning (Him); Aura Balancing and Strengthening (Him); Fringed Violet (Bush) – cleanses, heals and protects; Painini'Awa'Awa/Alo – heals holes; Protection (Aloha); Urchin (Pa) – protects; Yarrow (several versions) – protects; Guardian (Alaskan). **Sprays:** Angel Rejuvenation (Star Flower Essences); Aura Protection (Korte); Crystal Clear (Petal).

Crystals for the Aura

Amber (purifies and aligns); amethyst (aligns and protects); bloodstone (cleanses); citrine (aligns and cleans); labradorite (protects against 'leaks' and aligns to spiritual energy); lodestone (aligns); quartz (cleanses and strengthens); selenite (detaches entities); tourmaline (protects).

FIVE

THE Chakras

The chakras are, amongst other things, linkage points between the aura and the physical body. Seen clairvoyantly, they may look like a whirling vortex of energy depending on how open or closed they are. Traditionally the chakras have been described as a lotus flower – when closed, they look like a tightly-furled bud. There are many chakras on the body but the main ones rise up the spine from the base chakra at the perineum to the crown chakra at the top of the head (see illustration of The Chakras, Levels of Being and Aura Connections on page 45). If a chakra is open all the time, then energy leakage or psychic vampirism can occur at the level at which the chakra operates — emotional, physical, mental or spiritual.

The chakras correlate to different levels of being and to the various auric bodies. However, chakra interaction is subtle and complex. Emotional or mental processes may well affect chakras not directly related to that level of being, such as the base chakra, for instance, being affected by thought or fantasy.

Planes of Being

As human beings, we live in a physical body on the earth, but as we have seen, we also interact on mental, psychic and emotional levels. However, we need to remember that, as spiritual beings, we also inhabit other realms of being. Realms that we tend to be unaware of, until we raise our consciousness to reach them, as in meditation – or until one of the inhabitants of these worlds makes contact with us.

The Lower Astral Plane is the one closest to the earth. The term 'closest' indicates that it is vibrating at a rate near to that of the earth – rate of vibration being what distinguishes the different levels. It is to the lower astral plane that most souls travel immediately after death, and the majority of communication that is received from beyond death comes from this plane. Strong desires, either by 'the deceased' or their family, may keep people trapped at this level of being, as can ignorance and lack of awareness that physical death has actually taken place.

Experiences in the lower astral may be much like those on earth, until the 'deceased' recognizes that things can be different. Most people do not magically and immediately drop their personality and prejudices when they pass to the lower astral plane. So interaction with this plane tends to be characterized by the same desires and misconceptions as on the earth plane. However, there are souls who are able to work from beyond death to help the living. These souls may have chosen to inhabit the lower astral as it makes contact with the physical plane easier for them, but they are not tied to this plane and can move to the higher spiritual planes when appropriate.

On the Greek island of Zakynthos, in the cathedral in the main town, is the ornate silver coffin of Saint Dionysius (Dennis). He died over 200 years ago and his mummified body is on view to the faithful. He is one of many Greek saints who had healing powers while alive, and who is believed to continue that healing work today. Whilst alive, he would appear to people who were ill – his body remaining at his monastery. He is still seen at the bedside of the sick and, on such occasions, people visiting his tomb find that the saint is 'out' – there is a definite change in the atmosphere of the chapel in which his body is kept. Icons of Saint Dionysius are said to be efficacious not only for healing but also for protection. A German couple whose car was wrecked in a car crash on the island, but were themselves unhurt, were immediately hurried off to give thanks to Saint Dionysius for their safe delivery. The older inhabitants of the island would not dream of starting out on a journey without asking the protection of the saint.

This Greek tradition of journeying out of the body to heal the sick continues today. Daskalos, known as the Magus of Strovolos, was a contemporary healer who, whilst alive, appeared all over the island of Cyprus. Since his death, he has widened his work and appears to those who work with him all around the world. In his teaching Daskalos said that what he called the psychonoetic world existed side by side with the physical world and that it was 'everywhere and yet nowhere'. For him, as for the ancient Egyptians, it was quite natural that those who inhabited these other planes could and would communicate with the world of the living until they were ready to proceed onto higher planes of vibration.

Out-of-body Experience

Consciousness leaving the physical body behind and travelling in a subtle-body (the ancient Egyptian ka or etheric body) to different planes of being – or to other places on the earth. Out-of-body experiences can take place during sleep, meditation, near-death experiences and times of shock and trauma.

Thought forms and elemental beings also inhabit the lower astral realm – which is why it is dangerous territory for the unwary. Many of the beings to be found here are mischievous and untrustworthy (elemental spirits and the like), some of whom have evil intent (often called 'demonic beings'). Such beings may have been formed from the powerful thoughts and desires of those who left the earth plane some time ago but they can also be created by people living today. Or these entities may have been attracted by such thoughts (see page 72). If you venture into this realm unprepared, then you are likely to encounter problems. For instance, when first learning meditation, it can be quite usual to see all kinds of faces 'leering' at you, and to experience a most unpleasant atmosphere. Meditators quickly learn to pass beyond this scary place, but you can unwittingly 'bring back' something nasty that attaches to your aura and continues to affect you psychically. Which is why it makes sense to meditate in a safe space and to ground yourself fully in your body when you return to everyday consciousness.

It is to the lower astral realm that people tend to go when 'out of their body'. It can be consciously directed or happen spontaneously, but the person may be totally unaware of it. This state can occur during sleep or meditation but may also be experienced during periods of deep emotional shock or trauma (see page 110). Near-death experiences are invariably described from a vantage point above and the person reports looking down on the physical body either at the beginning or end of the experience. People with a tendency to be out of their physical body most of the time (in other words, ungrounded) are particularly open to psychic possession and the like because of their close association with the lower astral realm.

Souls progress to the **Higher Astral Plane** as the personality and the emotions drop away. Here the soul prepares either to move to the **Spiritual Planes,** once ingrained mental patterns, desires and beliefs have disintegrated; or for a rebirth on the earth plane. Communication with the higher astral level is still possible from earth, and some channelings will be from this plane. Communication with the spiritual planes is more difficult, but is the aim of most spiritual practices. Guides and spiritual teachers who guard and guide those still on earth usually reside on the spiritual planes (but it is not wise to assume that all so-called 'spiritual' communication will come from this level). This is also a realm of angels and angelic protection.

Channelling

Information passed to the earth plane via someone now living on earth (a channel) from discarnate sources – some of whom claim to be extra-terrestrial, others guides who once lived on earth.

The Chakras and Levels of Being

The **root** or **earth chakra** below the feet is concerned with grounding the physical. This chakra actually needs to be open most of the time as it holds you within physical incarnation and grounds you in your body. If this chakra is permanently closed, then you cannot operate in the here and now of everyday reality. However, if you are in a place where the earth energies are unbalanced or negative, then you need to be aware of that and close the earth chakra until the energies improve. If you are not aware, then you can easily pick up negative energies that will stay with you when you leave. It is important that the earth chakra is fully opened following meditation, healing or other consciousness expanding activities as this prevents unwanted interference or energy leeching by grounding you back into your physical body and sealing the aura.

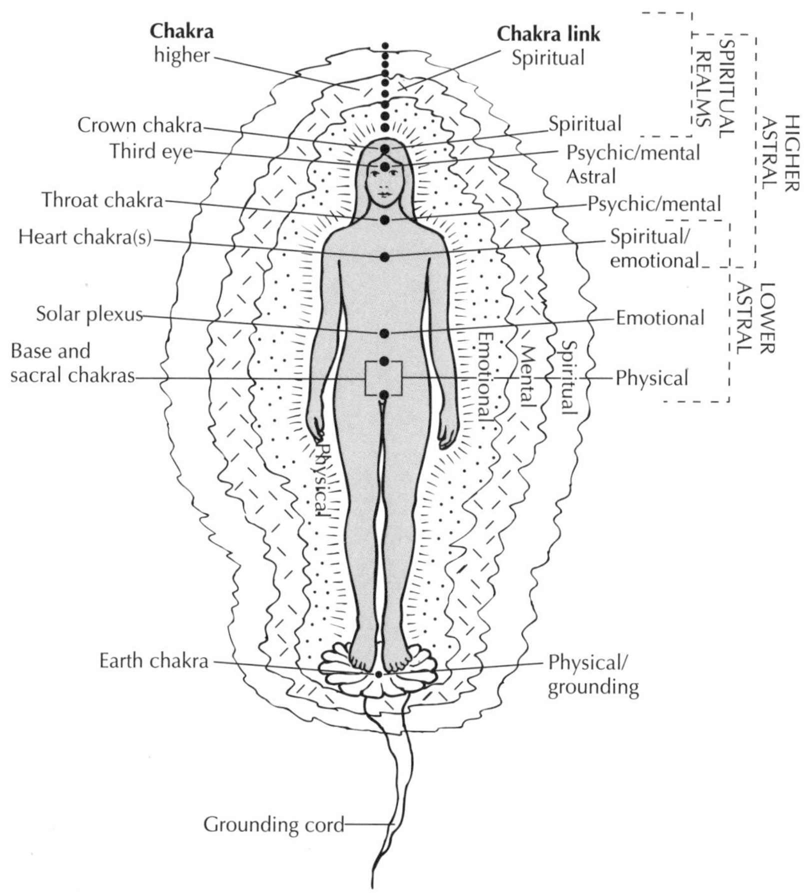

The Chakras, Levels of Being and Aura Connections

The **base** and **sacral chakras** are also concerned with the physical level but may be the site of 'emotional hooks' from another person. This is where you are open to another person through sexual contact – which may not always occur in a physical way. Psychic rape – that is, someone else having strong sexual fantasies or thoughts about you – can also adversely affect these chakras and it is not unusual to find a parent 'hooked' in their child's lower chakras through incestuous feelings or actual abuse. However, strong emotional feelings about a child that are not overtly or covertly sexual may still 'hook' into these chakras simply from the intensity of the feeling or the mental beliefs from the parent – guarding a daughter's virginity, for example. Such 'hooks' or attachments can then leave the child open to attachment from someone else in the future who brings up those feelings. Incestuous feelings, and indeed sexual feelings generally, can form part of the repressed and denied shadow part of our psyche. This shadow lurks in the depths of the unconscious and can rise up to, seemingly, 'attack' us through another person or circumstances.

The lower chakras have a natural connection with the lower astral and spirits inhabiting this realm can interact with the living through them. If these chakras are stuck open, then it is also possible for entities from the lower astral levels to become attached – or for beings who have made the transition to these levels from the earth to remain attached.

Psychic Rape

Strong sexual thoughts or fantasies which affect the object of those thoughts at a psychic level in exactly the same way that a physical rape would do.

The **solar plexus** and the **heart chakras** are concerned with the emotional level of being and therefore have a connection with the lower astral realm. The heart chakra can also be connected to the spiritual planes through unconditional love. These chakras, especially the solar plexus, are linked to where we store our old emotions and where we keep the buttons to reactivate them. This storage space is out of sight in our subconscious mind but the colours of those emotions will show in both the chakra and the auric body associated with it. Another person may knowingly or unknowingly press one of these buttons and bring about a reaction out of all proportion to the event – a sign that an old emotion has been triggered. If these old emotions are not released, then we are prone to both invasion and psychic leeching through these chakras and the emotional triggers connected with them.

The **higher heart chakra** is located above the heart. Its opening and activation indicates a shift to a more spiritual perspective. It is the chakra of unconditional love and can act as a protector for the heart. (The crystal **dioptase** helps to open this chakra as does the Alaskan **Kunzite** gem essence.) This chakra is attuned to the higher spiritual planes and should be open when you connect with this level.

The **throat** and **brow chakras** work at a more mental level and in addition are concerned with psychic states. The throat chakra particularly is connected with the higher astral plane and family belief patterns that may linger there. A blocked throat chakra can indicate a difficulty in communication – especially not being able to speak out. A blockage here means that someone is vulnerable to psychic invasion or manipulation through words and ideas – what you have been told you ought to believe, for instance, rather than what you have come to believe for yourself.

For many people, apparent psychic attack comes from outgrown and outworn beliefs that are nevertheless held onto – albeit unknowingly – until something brings them to consciousness again. But psychic attack may also be the result of an argument or conflict around beliefs (see page 130) especially by someone who believes they have a right to dictate how and what you will believe. If you feel that someone 'has you by the throat' (the Bailey essence Oxalis frees this up), then it is the throat chakra that shows the damage inflicted. At a psychic level, the attack or leakage may come from unvoiced intuitions or from communications which are seemingly at a spiritual level but which are actually from an unconscious, emotional source within yourself, or from your own fixed mental patterns. It is at this level that inherited 'family patterns' may manifest and masquerade as psychic attachment or an attack that appears to be from outside yourself.

If the **third eye** or **brow chakra** is stuck open, then you are vulnerable to the thoughts, feelings and influences not only of people around you on the earth level, but also on the astral level – and most especially the lower astral. This can feel like being bombarded constantly with thoughts and feelings that are not your own. You may also constantly receive 'psychic messages' as you will not be able to filter these out. You may be prey to wild psychic intuitions, premonitions of doom and the like – not all of which will come from outside yourself. A low-level astral entity can attach through this chakra and communicate with or through you. Such an entity may well masquerade as a highly-evolved spiritual being who is here to channel information of great importance to the world. Scepticism and questioning are one of your best defences against this, as is cleansing and closing the brow chakra and working psychically only when in a safe space.

Astral Entities

Entities that inhabit the astral realm may be departed souls that once lived on earth, but not necessarily so. This realm holds thought forms, elementals and what some people call demonic beings.

The **crown chakra** at the top of the head connects to the spiritual level of being as do the **higher chakras** above the head. People with these chakras stuck open will be ungrounded and may be unable to earth the high spiritual connection they make. (The Bush flower essence **Red Lily** cleanses the root chakra and opens the crown to ground spiritual energies in the body). If these chakras are not under your conscious control, then they may connect with the astral realms. After any kind of spiritual activity, it is important to check these chakras, close them and protect them within the aura.

The ideal situation is for all the chakras to be balanced and able to open and close at will, under your conscious control.

The Chakras and Meditation

When meditating, healing or journeying, it is helpful to open all the chakras systematically from the base of the spine up and ensure that the root and base chakras remain open so that you ground your spiritual activity in your physical body. After meditation, closing the chakras from the top down to the base, leaving the earth chakra open brings you back into the everyday world.

The Chakras and Psychic Invasion

The illustration below shows what happens when the crown and brow chakras are stuck open (especially if they have been 'blown open' by drugs or incorrectly supervized spiritual practices). It is like having a light beacon on the top of your head, to which all kinds of entities can be attracted. Through the chakras' contact with the lower astral realm, you are wide open to psychic invasion, but the light may reach onto other planes of being and attract entities from that level. Unless these entities are worked with consciously, and checked out first, psychic havoc can ensue just as easily as when those from the lower astral attach.

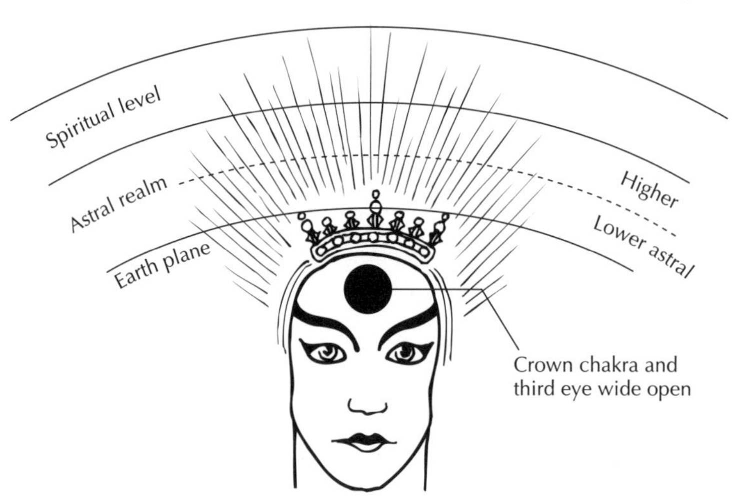

The Planes of Being and the Light Beacon

Many people are open to psychic invasion simply because one or more of the chakras are 'stuck' open and therefore unprotected. (The flower essence **Bush Iris** helps to balance blocked chakras). Intense emotions can affect both the heart and the solar plexus chakras but can have a 'knock-on' effect to the throat chakra. Sexual encounters can adversely affect the two lower chakras and powerful meditation or drug experiences can 'blow' the crown or brow chakras. It is also possible for other people to affect, and in a sense remain within, a chakra. A chakra tie clearing exercise can be most useful here, as can flower essences.

One of the basic lessons in psychic protection is to monitor and control the opening and closing of the chakras, to bring them under conscious direction of your will. There are times when it will be appropriate to have a chakra open, and times when it will be appropriate for it to be closed. Learning the difference between the two states is the start of the process, assessing which is appropriate in any given situation is the next stage, and automatically monitoring and controlling your chakras is the ultimate aim.

Checking the Chakras

If you find it difficult to visualize your chakras or to check whether they are open or closed, a pendulum can be used to dowse the energy. However, it is possible to train yourself to see or sense chakras, which can be accessed from the front or back of the body. Chakras that are fully open tend to be exceptionally bright, rotating at a fast rate and may feel hot and energized. Chakras that are closed have much less light, and may appear as dark shadows. They tend to rotate slowly and may feel cold and energy-less. Sometimes chakras appear to spin in opposite directions as you move from one to another, but this is not necessarily the case. It is also possible to feel the energies with the palm of your hand. You will probably feel a tingling when the chakra is open and may find that one particular chakra is sending out much more, or much less energy, than the others, indicating an imbalance (a chakra which is too open in relation to the others is just as much an imbalance as one that is too closed). It is also useful to notice whether you instinctively cover one of your chakras – such as the throat or solar plexus – with your hand when you are with a particular person.

When using a pendulum to check your chakras, it is probable that you will find the pendulum rotates at a different speed according to whether the chakra is open or closed. A fast spin usually indicates an open chakra. It is sensible to check this by specifically asking the question: 'Does this indicate an open chakra' once you have established your 'yes' and 'no' answers from the pendulum. Some people find that the pendulum spins or rotates in different directions for yes and no, other people find that a circle is 'yes' and a backwards and forwards motion is 'no'. (The quickest way to ascertain which is your particular indication is to put the pendulum over the palm of the hand which is not holding the pendulum and ask 'Is my name Joe Bloggs'. The movement of the pendulum will indicate 'no'. Then give your correct name and you will find your 'yes'.)

Exercise: Chakra Shutters

Sitting comfortably in an upright chair, close your eyes and establish a gentle breathing rhythm. Encase yourself in a light bubble to protect your energy.

Take your attention down to the base of your spine. Visualize a whirling vortex of energy and then picture a pair of shutters closing over the spot, shutting out the light. Practise opening and closing these shutters a few times until it becomes automatic. (You will be able to sense the difference within your body as the chakra opens and closes.)

Then bring your attention to the sacral chakra immediately below your navel. Picture this as full of light, and then close the shutters across. Open and close this chakra until it is automatic.

Then bring your attention up to your solar plexus and once more visualize the chakra open, and then close it off with the shutters.

Move on up to the heart chakra, opening and closing it a few times. (You may also be able to sense the higher heart chakra, in which case practise opening and closing this as well.)

Then take your attention to your throat and check this chakra. Open and close it before moving up to the brow chakra (above and between your eyebrows), and finally move to the top of your head for the crown chakra.

Once you are confident you can open and close the chakras at will, practise running your mind up and down your spine to assess the state of your chakras.

Before you bring your attention back into the room, take your mind to the ground underneath your feet. A short distance below your feet is the earth chakra. Sense whether this is open or closed and practise shutting it. Before completing the exercise, make sure your earth chakra is open and functioning well.

Bring your attention fully back into the room. Then stand up and feel your feet firmly on the floor. Have a good stretch and breathe deeply to ground yourself once more.

Note: You may find other chakras, in which case practise opening and closing these too.

If you find it difficult to visualize, you can use your hands to simulate the opening and closing of the chakra shutters until you can sense the difference between an open and closed chakra.

Exercise: Chakra Cleansing

Repeat the exercise above, this time checking out the colour and spin of each chakra in turn. If the chakra looks murky or has dark patches, visualize light entering the chakra to cleanse it. See the light whirling round until all the blackness is cleared. When you have finished, all the chakras should have an equal brightness and energy intensity. Complete the exercise by opening the earth chakra and closing the chakras along the spine and head. Then bring your attention fully back into the room. Feel your feet on the floor and be aware of your connection with the earth. Breathe deeply and have a good stretch to remind yourself that you are fully present in your body.

Exercise: Clearing Chakric Ties

This exercise cuts off any source of energy depletion from another person – and also releases anyone whom you might be psychically vampirizing or holding onto for any reason. It can be useful to do this exercise to check out your connection with your child or your partner – or an ex-partner. It does not cut off any unconditional love there may be between you but it can prevent inappropriate energy loss. If you are afraid that doing this exercise will cut off the 'love' between you, then it may be helpful for you to question the kind of 'love' you have. Is it, perhaps, dependent or collusive? Manipulation, possession, control, domination, energy leeching and feeding off each other all masquerade as 'love'. Such control or dependence creates a vulnerability which leaves one or the other person open to psychic control and depletion.

Unconditional love implies freedom: the freedom to be oneself and to allow the other person to be in exactly the space they need. It does not mean knowing 'what is best for them' or getting one's own needs met through that person. Nor does it involve becoming a 'victim to love' (which is extremely weakening at a psychic and emotional level). When 'loving' there is a choice. You can love unconditionally, which is life enhancing and invigorating for you both; or you can love conditionally with 'oughts, shoulds and expectations' attached, which is draining and life denying – and which invokes a need for psychic protection.

To do the following exercise, choose a time and place where you will not be disturbed. If necessary, switch off the phone and put a note on the door that you are unavailable. It is important that you complete this exercise in one go and do the healing work at the same time.

Seat yourself comfortably and allow your body to relax.

Begin by creating a safe space for yourself. Visualize a pyramid that completely encloses your space, be it a house, a flat, or a room. The pyramid can be of any colour or material that feels good to you. It has four sides and a floor. Then use bright white light to sweep out the inside of the pyramid so that it is clean and fresh. (This pyramid can also be used as a personal protector.)

Choose the space in which to do this work. You may like to use the room you are in, but you can also picture yourself in a garden or a meadow, by the sea or in some other place where you feel safe and good. Picture this place, strongly, bringing it alive in your mind. You will need a large, flat space and a place to have a fire.

Mark out your space by drawing a circle around you at arms length on the ground. You can use light, chalk, paint or whatever feels right. In front of that circle, but not touching it, draw another circle.

Now ask that anyone who has an inappropriate chakra tie connection with you will appear in the circle. (If you know who it is beforehand, you can put them there to begin with. If there are more than one, take each one in turn or leave some until another day.)

Check out whether that chakra connection is appropriate. Some chakric connections are positive and nurturing but you may well find a connection that is inappropriate and depleting for you. If this is the case, ask to be shown which chakra(s) the inappropriate connection links into. You may well see that as hooking into one or more chakra with a connection back to the other person. You may also find that a piece of that person is lodged in one of your chakras, or part of you is in one of theirs.

Now remove the connection. Take as much time as you need. You may find that you need a scalpel, a light laser or some other tool to aid you. Ask that whatever you need will be given to you. When you have removed it from yourself, heal and seal the place with light. Then remove it from the other person. (Pile up any connections outside the circle as you work).

Check all your other chakras in case there is a further entanglement. If there is, clear that.

If you find that you are holding onto part of another person, give that part back willingly and with love. If you find that another person is holding part of you, ask that they return that part willingly and with love. (If this does not work, use your will to take that part back. You may have to ask if they need you to do something for them first. If it is something that is within your power, and which does not disempower you or deplete you further, then carry out this request. If it is not appropriate, say so.)

When you are sure that you have cleared all the chakric ties, wrap healing light around yourself, and another light around the other person, and let them go with unconditional love and forgiveness. If it is appropriate, receive their forgiveness also. Move them back out of your space and into their own space.

If you have other people to work with, do each one in turn (if time is short, move onto the next stage and leave the other people until another time.)

Now take your attention to the chakric ties that you piled up outside the circle. Put them all into a big, blazing bonfire and allow the fire to transmute and purify the energy. When all the ties have been consumed, take back the transmuted energy into yourself and let it energize and heal you. (You can either take it back into the chakra from which the tie came, or use it to energize your aura.)

Check that all your chakras are open and balanced. Then close them carefully with the exception of the earth chakra. Wrap yourself in a light bubble for protection.

Slowly bring your attention back into the room and, when you are ready, open your eyes. Breathe deeply and allow yourself to be fully present in your physical body. Get up and move around.

It can be extremely beneficial to spray both yourself and the room in which you carried out this exercise with **Crystal Clear** (Petal) to complete the clearing.

(The above exercise can also be used to disconnect your energies from another person in a more general way. It will cut off any expectations, 'oughts and shoulds', karmic ties and inappropriate demands. Instead of asking for the chakric connections to be shown, ask for any inappropriate ties to be shown wherever they are located.)

Exercise: The Grounding Cord

A useful way of grounding yourself in your physical body is to imagine that you are connected through the earth chakra to a root which goes deep into the centre of the earth. Before undertaking this exercise, check out the earth energies around you – using a pendulum if necessary. If the earth energies are contaminated, leave your earth chakra closed and clean those energies first – **Crystal Clear** (Petal) may be all you need but see page 89.

Stand with your feet firmly on the floor and take your attention down to your feet. Close your eyes.

A short distance below your feet, there is an earth chakra which looks like a large, open flower. Try to sense whether this chakra is open or closed. (If you sense that this chakra is not open, then open it before proceeding further.)

Picture a root or grounding cord growing from the bottom of each of your feet. It passes into the centre of the flower where the two strands unite. The root then goes deep down into the earth. It is flexible and allows you to move around, but it holds you firmly in incarnation.

This root reaches right into the molten centre of the earth and allows you to draw energy up the root, through the soles of your feet, and on up into your body where you can store it just below your navel. Spend a few moments breathing into that part of your belly and allowing the energy to move up the root and through your lower body to that spot below the navel — which may feel hot and energized.

When you are fully energized, and feel firmly grounded within your physical body, open your eyes and bring your attention fully back into the room.

Alaskan **Black Tourmaline** and **Ruby** gem essences strengthen the connection between the base chakra and the earth and can be taken before commencing the exercise.

Flower Essences for the Chakras

Chakra set (Aid, Him, Korte); Araryba (Arare) – opens chakras 1–4 and Celebracao (Arare) – opens chakras 3, 5 and 7; Bush Iris (Bush) – cleanses blockages; Red Lily (Bush) – cleanses root and opens crown; A'Ali'I (Aloha) – cleanses heart chakra of blockages associated with past relationships; Kou (Aloha) stimulates brow chakra; Kunzite (Alaskan) opens higher heart chakra; Fringed Violet and Flannel Flower combination (Bush) – close down.

Crystals for opening and protecting the Chakras

Base and sacral: azurite, bloodstone, chrysocolla, obsidian, golden topaz, black tourmaline.
Solar plexus: malachite, jasper, tigers eye.
Heart: rose quartz, amazonite, adventurine.
Higher Heart: Dioptase.
Throat: azurite, turquoise, amazonite, aquamarine, blue topaz, blue tourmaline.

Brow: sodalite, moldavite, azurite, herkimer diamond, lapis lazuli, azurite.

Crown: moldavite, citrine, quartz.

Grounding energy from crown to base chakra: smoky quartz.

Opening and cleansing all: amber.

Aligning: boji.

Elevating: turquoise.

SIX

PSYCHIC PROTECTION in Everyday Life

Many people believe that psychic protection is not for them because they have not upset anyone, or 'do not do anything weird'. They assume that because they do not see ghosts or are not intuitive they are not open to the psychic realm. However! It can be in the small, everyday things of life that psychic protection is most needed, and yet not practised.

You may not realize how objects such as letters, photographs and gifts can tie you to someone after the relationship has finished. If there was any acrimony or power struggle in that relationship, then the objects still carry that charge. Even when the relationship finished on good terms, there might be hidden links. For this reason, it is wise to regularly clear out such things, either giving them away to a charity shop or jumble sale, or burning them if this is more appropriate. If you are keeping them, then cleansing them with an appropriate essence or putting a crystal on them will diminish the possibility of anything still being attached to you through them – or of someone else holding onto a part of you. (If you come under psychic attack from someone, then it is essential to get rid of any gifts they gave you, or objects belonging to them as this makes strong links for them to reach you through.)

If you do come under psychic attack or experience undue influence from someone, then you are usually aware of this and of the need to defend yourself. But you may ignore the more subtle effect of thoughts, feelings, atmospheres – and relationships. You may also not realize that the exhaustion you feel, the physical, mental or emotional depletion you suffer, is because you have given too much of yourself to someone else.

Giving Yourself Away

'Giving away of oneself' can occur at work, at play and in relationships. Whenever you become aware of being depleted after being with a particular person, then it is worth asking yourself:

- Have I given too much of myself?
- Did I remember to detach myself after our contact finished?
- Have I taken on something from that person?
- Am I allowing someone else to have undue influence over me?
- Am I taking enough time for me?

You may also like to ask yourself:

- Do particular places affect me?
- Do I get depleted when I travel on a bus or train?
- Do I always sit in the same place and then feel tired?

Throughout this book, you will find ways of dealing with all these situations. For now, it is enough to have noted that this occurs, and with whom it happens.

Then ask yourself some questions about boundaries.

- Do I take on too much?
- Do people overburden me with their troubles?
- Do I feel overwhelmed by other peoples' emotions or thoughts?
- Am I able to say no?
- Can I take sufficient time for myself?

If you are unable to stand in your own space, within a strong boundary, then you may need some counselling to gently support you as you make changes in your way of approaching the world.

Now ask yourself how you feel in your body:

- Do I feel earthed and grounded?
- Am I practical or airy-fairy?
- Do people describe me as 'feet on the ground' or 'standing on tiptoe?'
- Do I breathe right down into my belly or am I a shallow breather (which can be a symptom of chronic anxiety and stress)?

Take a few experimental breaths that pull air deep down inside you.

- How does it feel?
- How was it when you checked your aura?
- Were you all over the place, or was your aura strong?

If you are not fully present in your body, then some bodywork or yoga might be helpful in supporting the psychic protection you are giving yourself. You may also need help to retrieve the parts of yourself that you have given way.

Protection Whilst Travelling

If you feel depleted after travelling in the company of other people, cross your ankles and your wrists – this seals your energy circuit. You can also picture yourself in a psychic space suit, use appropriate protection essences or wear a **labradorite** crystal around your neck. If you have a long flight **Travel Essence** (Bush) taken at regular intervals keeps your energies balanced. Spraying with **Crystal Clear** (Petal) and a little lavender oil keeps the space around you clear and refreshed.

Turning Down the Volume

Psychic protection can be useful in other ways too. Say you go out for the evening. You want a nice, quiet, romantic time. But the people at the next table are talking loudly, the kind of conversation that everyone has to listen to because of its sheer volume. Well, you do not have to listen. Simply imagine a tall, glass bell jar. The sort that used to be put around precious items on display, or that covered tender plants in winter. Mentally pop it over the couple and have it block out all the sound. Within a few moments you will have forgotten all about them and can enjoy your evening. This visualization works well with mobile phone users too – as does a 'psychic volume control' that you mentally turn down whenever someone gets too loud. Bell jars are good for blocking off disturbing energies too. If someone next to you is agitated or angry – or if they are clearly suffering from a cold or flu – pop a bell jar over them. If you can spray **Crystal Clear** (Petal) around, so much the better.

Psychic Protection and Sleep

When you are asleep, your defences are down. You are at your most open, especially if you leave your body at night (as many people do during dream and deep sleep states). At a physical level, you may be vulnerable through the astrological composition of your birthchart to energy loss to another person. But this can work at an emotional or mental level too. Certain people can 'drain you', especially when you are sleeping. This can be particularly so if you share a bed with that person.

The energy loss may be linked to the element balance in your birthchart. Someone who is 'fiery' will 'burn up' or consume the energy of, say, someone who is 'watery'. That is, someone who has many planets in the fire element could draw energy from someone who has several planets in water. On the other hand, water puts out fire, so a 'watery' person may well quench the energy of a fire sign. (Aries, Leo and Sagittarius are fire signs, Taurus, Virgo and Capricorn earth signs, Gemini, Libra and Aquarius air signs, and Cancer, Scorpio and Pisces water signs. There are eleven astrological planets and these can be distributed between the different elements in numerous combinations, creating different imbalances.)

Nevertheless, there can be many different reasons for energy loss while you sleep. If the energy loss is severe and linked to your partner, then it might be sensible to sleep in separate beds but you can safeguard your energy through essences, visualization or crystals once you are aware of the problem. It only takes a moment or two before going to bed to strengthen your aura but it is well worth establishing as a nightly ritual, especially if you suffer from insomnia or wake up feeling more tired than when you went to bed.

Most people are now familiar with Feng Shui, the Chinese art of arranging a harmonious environment in accordance with carefully laid down principles. Feng Shui can be a useful aid to sleeping in a safe space. As this art is based on the free flow of *chi* or *Qi*, it is considered most unwise to sleep with the head of your bed immediately behind a door as this cuts off *Qi*. The most auspicious place is cater-corner to the door; that is, on the wall facing the door but off

to one side so that the door does not open on to the bed. Mirrors are also used extensively in Feng Shui. Positioned correctly, they can repel evil spirits and draw in positive energies (a practitioner should be consulted for precise placements). A mirror should not be placed so that the occupants of a bed can see themselves in it – particularly at the foot of the bed. If they can, they are likely to suffer from insomnia and disturbed dream-sleep as it weakens physical energy and creates disharmony in the subtle energy bodies. The Chinese believe that, during sleep, the subtle energy bodies, housed within the etheric body, can leave the physical body and move around independently. A mirror in the wrong position confuses the etheric body when it tries to return to the physical body. Moving the bed or mirror can bring relief.

Many people experience 'out-of-body' states during sleep and many dreams are, in fact, 'memories' of out-of-body experiences. Lucid dreams (that is a dream where you know you are dreaming and can direct the dream) usually take you out of your body. Your etheric body may need protection at this time.

Flower Essences for Protection During Sleep
Yarrow and White Violet (Alaskan); Fringed Violet (Bush); Araryba (Arare). **Nightmares:** Dog Rose (Bush); Panini-O-Ka (Aloha).

A Daily Ritual

If you have become aware that you are psychically vulnerable in your day to day life, then you can create a simple daily protection ritual for yourself. Set aside five or ten minutes each morning and find a combination of solutions which work for you. An example might be to check your aura and crystallize the edges (see page 36) and then to take a psychic protection essence to lock this into place. You could follow this up by wearing a protective crystal. This would work well if you have become aware that you are like a psychic sponge, soaking up everything around you. If, on the other hand, you are aware of low energy levels, then ten or twenty minutes daily of Qi Gong, Yoga or Tai Chi Chuan would strengthen your Qi (the defensive, energizing force which flows in your body). You could follow this up with an essence to support your lower chakras. You might also find that a slow release carbohydrate breakfast such as porridge or unsweetened muesli helps to protect your energies.

At the end of the day, it is equally important to have a daily ritual to cleanse your energies. You could use a visualization of light sweeping down through your body, or you could spray yourself with **Crystal Clear** or put this in your bath. If you have been listening to people all day and could have taken on their thoughts or feelings, then you can visualize these being transmuted by the light or the **Crystal Clear** into clear, positive energies. You could also hold a suitable crystal in your hands such as an **Apache Tear** or **Smoky Quartz** and allow all the energies you are holding onto to flow into that crystal for transmutation and cleansing.

A useful exercise to do before sleeping is to review the day to see if you are holding onto thoughts or resentments about other people. If you are, then consciously let the thought or feeling go and let forgiveness go to that person – and to yourself. This helps to keep your energies clear and to avoid any hooks that might be created for psychic attachment or attack at some time in the future.

Invoking the Angel of Protection

Part of your daily ritual could include invoking your angel of protection. Everyone has a guardian angel to watch over them and the more conscious you are of this contact, the more protection you will receive. Invoking this angel is also useful if you are walking in a dark or dangerous place, if you have a particularly hard task to perform, if you are opening up psychically in an unknown energy space, or if you are meeting someone with whom there is a conflict. But, as with everything to do with psychic protection, it is no use waiting until you need your angel before you try to make contact.

Exercise: Meeting the Angel of Protection

Spend a few moments relaxing, breathing gently and evenly and letting any tension flow out of your body through your hands and feet.

When you are ready, picture a shaft of light coming down in front of you. This shaft of light reaches from the angelic realms down to the earth plane. Ask that your Angel of Protection will travel down this shaft of light to meet you.

When your angel arrives, feel it move to stand behind, wrapping you in protective wings. Spend as long as you like with your angel, building up trust and enjoying the sense of protection. Ask your angel to be with you whenever you need protection. Affirm to yourself that this will be so.

Ask your angel to show you a 'call sign', something you only need think about to have your angel present. Ask your angel to leave and practise calling a few times so that you will know that your angel will come when you have need.

Then thank your angel for being there. The shaft of light will then recede back to the angelic realms.

Before opening your eyes, check that your aura is enclosed in a bubble of light and that the earth chakra beneath your feet is open and grounding you. Then, when you are ready, bring your attention fully back into the room and open your eyes.

Flower Essences for Angelic Contact

Angel of Protection (Korte); Angelsword (Bush); Bromelia 2 (Arare); Chiming Bells and Kunzite (Alaskan); Calling all Angels (Alaskan).

Crystals for Angelic Contact

Celestite (particularly angelite); selenite; muskovite; aquamarine; danburite; morganite.

Who's Been Sleeping in Your Bed?

Another subtle, but vital, need is to protect yourself when sleeping in a strange bed, as the following case history from David Eastoe shows:

CASE HISTORY: STALE HOTEL ROOM

After thousands of occupants, many of whom are not in a particularly positive state of mind, hotel rooms often get a really stale vibe going.

One such room in Japan also had an occupant in the form of a discarnate wartime soldier, who seemed really freaked out. Crystal Clear and an open window dispersed the worst of it, and the gentleman seemed to vanish too. I know a lot of people will suggest a more caring attitude toward the confused departed, but after a very long journey what one needs is a good night's sleep. The plant essences don't hurt such entities, and ghosts often leave for good, the energies which held them in place perhaps being dispersed, and they are able to 'move on'.

Personally, I always carry a Crystal Clear spray with me when I travel and spray both the room and bathroom, paying special attention to the bed, whenever I have to sleep away from home.

Geopathic Stress

Geopathic stress is characterized by a sense of unwellness (it is often an underlying cause of chronic diseases such as ME and cancer). 'Ghosts' and psychic entities are drawn to this energy, although they may be perfectly harmless. Strangely enough, people are often 'addicted' to geopathic stress and choose to put their favourite chair, or their bed, in a particularly stressed spot. Cats too love stressed spots. So, if your cat sleeps on your favourite chair, or your bed, then this can be an indication that it is in a geopathically stressed place. Moving the chair, or the bed, can be all that is needed – although you could well suffer from a headache or exacerbation of your symptoms while your body readjusts. However, you may need to get an expert in or to use a purpose-made device for clearing geopathic stress (see Appendix).

The Power of Thought

It is in the normal everyday world that the power of thought can be recognized. Thought is what brings things into being. It makes them manifest. What you expect to happen, happens. What you believe comes to pass. Indeed, you are what you believe. What you fear most is attracted towards you. If you give a thought energy, it becomes powerful. Once you fully understand the validity of this idea, you can use the power of thought to protect yourself. When you visualize a guardian angel, you are in effect constructing a thought form (see page 134). If you have an irrational belief, you can reprogramme it. If you have a fear, you can use the power of your mind to overcome it. If you believe you have no control over what happens to you, you can take charge of your life.

You can use the power of thought to change your focus. Withdrawing your energy, not focussing on something deflates it. It cannot continue unless you give it energy. So, stop dwelling on your fears or resentments, cease thinking about someone or something that is causing you trouble, desist from always expecting the worst, and your life will change for the better. This is especially so in cases of psychic attack but it can also work in psychic attachment and other instances.

The old precept 'like attracts like' is true. If you continuously put out fearful, anxious thoughts, what will come back to you will induce more fear. If you emanate envious, hateful or jealous feelings, what will come back will be envy, hate and jealousy. If you are in inner turmoil, what you will attract will be conflict. These things may occur at a psychic level or at a physical level. You can protect yourself by having good expectations and thinking 'beautiful thoughts'.

Negative Expectations

Not all psychic attack, or energy leeching, comes from outside ourselves. Thoughts, feelings and expectations, especially ones you are not aware of, can easily trip you up. If you fear the worst, then it will probably happen. And it may well manifest through objects associated with you – in subtle ways – as the following case history from soul retrieval and spirit release therapist Dawn Robins shows:

CASE HISTORY: SELF-UNDOING

'I was going to the vet, half expecting having to discuss whether it was time to put my dog down. She had belonged to my mother, who had died some years previously and so this was a particularly emotional decision.

'Within two hundred yards of leaving the house the car started misfiring and I drove for the next 20 minutes with the car cutting out and almost breaking down. As I entered the village where the vet lived, it totally cut out and died. I managed to coast down the hill to the door of the vet.

'After seeing the vet and her reassuring me that my dog's illness wasn't as serious as I thought, I went out to try the car before calling for help. It started first time and we sailed home with not a single splutter – showing that my mental attitude had been affecting the car. My not wanting to go and my fear were played out by the car.

'Sometime later, I was driving a friend to see a clairvoyant when the car started to play up again. I wondered out loud if someone was trying to prevent us from making the journey. "Oh, I hope so," she said, "I'm really scared of what she'll say." I suggested to my friend that her fear might be creating the situation with the car and asked her if, as she was so ambivalent about going, she thought she would get anything from the reading anyway. "Well," she said, "I know I need guidance as I cannot handle the situation in which I find myself. So, yes, I do want to go. I'll put my fear aside." With that, the car picked up and we had no further trouble.

'As a follow on, it occurred to me that if my negative thoughts – and those of a friend – can cause that to happen, then so can someone else's thoughts directed towards me. I began to use a pentagram to protect my car every time I went out and have had no further trouble.'

Protecting Your Car

Driving a car can be hazardous and with 'road rage' on the increase, it is important to protect yourself, your passengers and your car when travelling – and to protect any other form of transport you use. Here again, it is a question of 'like attracts like'. If you are an aggressive, impatient driver, then you are more likely to attract rage or minor accidents. But you may be angry without knowing it and may need to practise sending thoughts of love and peace to the idiot crawling along in front of you, to the traffic signals that hold you up, or the roadworks that block your path. If you have become angry at these, no matter how unconsciously, then you may well attract accidents. So, being calm aids being safe.

However, there are things that you can do before setting out from home to ensure that you arrive safely.

Traditionally, the god Mercury, or Hermes, is the god of travel. He has been invoked since time immemorial to aid travellers. Even today many people still ask for 'permission to travel' and may carry a small replica of the god with them for protection on journeys.

A Saint Christopher medal was used for this purpose for many years, until the saint was declared redundant. As with so much of psychic protection, it is not the actual object that works but the intention behind it. So, you can continue to use this or a similar object – I have a Tibetan mani stone which was given to me for that purpose but other cultures have comparable items imbued with a religious or protective energy.

The visualization below is an adaptation of an ancient one that is still effective today.

Exercise: Protecting Your Car (or Other Transport)

Before you start your car (or bike, plane, train or boat), close your eyes for a moment and mentally draw a pentagram in the air over the car. Ask that this will protect you and your car as you travel. (You can also draw a pentagram above the head of yourself and each passenger if conditions are particularly hazardous.)

> **Pentagram**
>
> *A five-pointed star imbued with protective energy*

The pentagram visualization can also be used if you have to park your car in an area where it might be subjected to vandalism or theft. Another useful way of protecting the car is to visualize it as invisible to thieves or vandals – but remember to make it visible again before you drive off so that other drivers can see you. (If you have to walk in dangerous areas, you can mentally place a pentagram above your head, or picture yourself 'cloaked in a dark garment' so that your light is not visible and you can walk safely.)

SEVEN

PROTECTING Your Space

The space in which you live and work needs cleansing and protection, just as much as you yourself. Its harmony can be affected by many things. Geopathic or electromagnetic stress, ghosts, psychic residues and the like all affect how safe your space is, as do the thoughts and feelings of those around you – and those who have gone before. As flower essence-maker David Eastoe explains:

> *Our homes and workspaces have an energy history. Everything which has taken place, not only in the buildings but on the land beneath them, will have left an impression which, if it is strong enough, may be felt in the present time. In The Tree of Life Israel Regardie explains how negative acts and emotions produce an accumulation of harmful energies on the etheric levels. As these build up, tension increases until there is the need of a discharge, which may take the form of an accident, an unpleasant act, or in more serious cases, a war, famine or natural disaster. On an everyday level, we may be affected in subtle ways by the energy in our surroundings, and it is important to keep these in a positive, clear state as much as possible.*

Electromagnetic Stress

Electromagnetic stress is caused by the subtle emanations of electrical, microwave and radio frequencies. It causes 'sick building syndrome', adversely affects the immune system and is implicated in cancer and degenerative diseases.

Psychic Residue

The energy imprints left behind at a location. Residues can arise from old emotions, thoughts, behaviour and experiences, and also from people who have died there.

If you have psychic or electromagnetic pollution in your home, or workplace, if your house is sited on a point of 'negative energy', or if there are stray entities around who should have moved on but have not, then you will pick this up at both a psychic and a physical level. These adverse energies will affect you whatever activities you undertake. Opening yourself up to meditate in such a space, or simply relaxing or daydreaming, can open you up to psychic invasion, energy leeching or even to psychic attack.

Symptoms of Psychic Invasion of Your Living Space

- Unusual or unpleasant smells, particularly of mould or decay
- Cold patches
- Animal or child is uneasy in a particular room
- Insomnia/disturbed sleep
- Light bulbs blow frequently
- Electrical apparatus malfunctions

If you recognize any of these symptoms, then you need to cleanse and protect your space.

You may also need to look at the geopathic energies in your living space. Do you come home from work, sit down and then feel exhausted for the rest of the evening? If so, were you exhausted before you walked through the door? Geopathic stress can be addictive. You may find that your favourite chair is in a geopathically stressed place. Moving the chair may be all you need to do, but your home may need the help of experts if it is seriously stressed (see Appendix).

Creating a Safe Space

A little further on, you will find useful ways of cleansing your space through plants, crystals and sound. Imagery is also a powerful tool in space clearing and protecting. The following meditation can be performed quickly, and can be used morning and evening, especially if you have other people in your home or your working space. It is also a helpful visualization for preparing a safe space in which to meditate or to heal or counsel. (You can erect, and clean the energies within, a pyramid in one room or around the whole house, whichever is appropriate for you.) The pyramid visualization can also be used when you are in a crowded space and need to protect your own energies, or when you feel there is a danger of psychic invasion or attack.

Exercise: The Pyramid Meditation

Sit quietly and comfortably, breathing gently. To aid the visualization, close your eyes and look up to the space above and between your eyebrows.

Imagine that you are sitting in the middle of a pyramid. This pyramid can be of any material and any colour that you wish. Remember that the pyramid should have a floor under your feet (below your earth chakra) as well as four sides that meet above your head.

Let the pyramid expand to encompass the room in which you are sitting. (If you wish to do the whole house, let it grow large enough for the house to be enclosed within it.)

When the pyramid is the right size, take your attention up to the apex. Picture a bright light coming in from the apex and shining all around the pyramid. Let this light sweep out the pyramid, transmuting any negative energies into positive ones. Then allow the light to heal and revitalize the space within the pyramid.

Slowly bring your attention back into your body and be aware that the room (or house) is now protected by the pyramid. Take your attention down to your feet and re-earth yourself by connecting your earth chakra deep down into the earth, allowing the grounding cord to pass through the base of the pyramid.

When you are ready, open your eyes and move around.

Psychic Protection in the Home

It makes sense to have the best possible energies within your home. This is not something you do once or twice. It needs to be done on a regular, preferably daily basis especially if you work at home. Many of the ideas in this book will help you to protect your home through simple daily cleansing and protection rituals. You may need to have geopathic stress checked out (see page 80) and you may have to neutralize electromagnetic stress (especially from computers and TV screens), or other environmental pollution, but on the whole psychic protection within the home is usually a matter of keeping the psychic energies clean. This can include being clear and direct in how you express your feelings, especially anger (lingering, festering resentment is a major cause of, apparent, psychic attack).

If you find that your energies are disturbed by neighbours, there are several things you can do to counteract this. One is to visualize a lead barrier between the houses that will not allow 'bad vibes' through. Another is to place a piece of crystal between the houses – a reflective crystal such as **black tourmaline** will return energies whilst a loving crystal such as **rose quartz** will send 'good wishes' to heal misunderstandings or calm aggression – whether directed at you or simply present in your neighbour's house. If noise from an adjoining property is a problem, a crystal placed on the party wall will help. If your neighbourhood is the problem, then place a large protective crystal outside your front door to deflect the energies – if the crystal has a point, as in **amethyst** or **quartz**, point this away from the house. Program the crystal to keep you and your home safe. Remember to cleanse the crystal frequently and spray outside the front door with **Crystal Clear** from time to time.

If you live near a nuclear power station, or within a fall-out zone from disasters such as Chernobyl, then it can be useful to clear your energies with **T.1** essence (Korte) – not to be confused with **Ti** essence (Aloha). (This is also appropriate after X-rays or spending time where X-rays, microwaves etc. pass through). **T.1** essence should not be taken by mouth, nor should it be kept near other essences as it neutralizes them.

To clear your energies using **T.1**, first sit with a bottle of Andreas Korte's **Delph** Essence between your bare feet. Hold a bottle of **T.1** essence over your crown chakra until you feel a shift of energy. Then slowly bring the bottle of **T.1** down the midline of your body, at your own speed, until you reach your feet. This should neutralize your energies but if you are in any doubt a flower essence practitioner should be consulted.

Flower Essences for Environmental Pollution
T.1 and Delph (Korte); Ti (FES and Aloha); Clearing and Releasing Formula (Desert); Radiation Essences (Bush); Yarrow Special Formula (FES); Crystal Clear (Petal); Environmental Set, Yarrow and Black Tourmaline (Alaskan).

Crystals for Environmental Pollution
Turquoise; malachite (if nuclear reactor in your vicinity).

Ghosts

You may find that you have particular house problems such as a resident ghost. A ghost may be a psychic imprint that has been left behind, rather like a photograph. But it may be a troubled spirit to whom much wrong was done in that place, or an entity that wants to make contact with the living – or one that simply has not realized it is dead. (If this is a spirit with a troubled past, then it will probably be necessary to bring in a psychic to hear the story and help the spirit on its way.)

If spraying with **Crystal Clear** does not work – and it usually does when the ghost is a psychic imprint rather than a discarnate entity (which needs **Astral Clear** dispersing through an oil-burner) – then you should call in a specialist. You will find help at your local Spiritualist church or Psychic or Metaphysical Centre as you may need to contact the entity to help it on its way. It is not enough merely to banish or exorcise such a spirit. Unless it is sent to where it can receive help, it will simply move on to bother someone else. Such spirits tend to be misplaced, 'lost', or held by a strong desire or unfinished business rather than 'evil' but they can give you a great deal of trouble so consult an expert.

Poltergeists

Poltergeists too can create problems. Some poltergeist activity may be from the lower astral realm so here again it is worth getting it checked out by an expert. However, teenage children do generate energy that flashes around the place and creates havoc. Some of this can be emotional in nature, some is the result of hormonal changes. Again this is really a job for an expert but that expert might turn out to be a child psychologist rather than a spirit medium. On the other hand, children do tend to be naturally psychic so it may be that a teenager needs to learn how to handle this energy properly – in which case a healer or psychic can help.

CASE HISTORY: POLTERGEIST, EVIL SPIRIT OR FRIGHTENED BOY?

Many years ago now, when I was first training as a healer and psychic, a teenage boy was brought to the local spiritualist church healing group for an 'exorcism'. His parents and the church's minister, were convinced that he was 'possessed by an evil spirit'. There had been a great deal of poltergeist activity in the house, and the teenager was exceedingly depressed and suicidal.

The church minister put his hands on the boy's shoulders and began the 'exorcism', repeatedly telling the spirit to be gone. I became aware of this spirit. He was very lost, a teenager of about the same age. He told me that he had been attracted to the boy because they shared many feelings. Some of the poltergeist activity was his, as he was trying to attract attention so that the boy would know he had company. But it was not him who was causing the boy to feel suicidal, nor were the more frenetic poltergeist manifestations anything to do with him.

I asked that his guides and guardian beings would come and take the spirit boy to the Light – the place he most wanted to go. He had been able to see it, and hear people calling him, but did not know how to get there. In the Light, he would receive healing and be able to look back at his life on earth and his choices for the future.

The minister, who had continued to exhort the 'evil spirit' to leave, pronounced that the 'exorcism' was complete, the spirit had gone. He did not think the boy would have any further trouble.

But the teenager did.

I was training to be a teacher at this time and went on a school visit. Here I met the boy again. He was feeling exactly the same and, as he said: 'Even more bereft, as I felt that spirit cared about me.' He went on to tell me that his parents, although sharing the same house, lived separate lives, one upstairs and one down, and never spoke to each other. The parents used him as an intermediary. His father kept a loaded shotgun beside his bed and more than once threatened to kill himself 'because of her'. Despairing, the boy had picked up the shotgun and threatened to kill himself instead. The energy in the house was, in his words, 'poisonous'. They were extremely angry with each other and that anger festered in the house, rising to peaks which coincided with the worst of the poltergeist activity – activity which frightened the teenager very much. I suggested to him that he should visualize a bright shiny new dustbin, into which he would jump at the first sign of trouble. We also worked on strengthening his aura and giving him protection on a day-to-day level. He quickly learnt the pyramid meditation to create a safe space in his bedroom, where he spent most of his time.

I knew the local educational psychologist was a sensitive and open-minded man with a particular interest in this kind of phenomenon and its causes, both psychic and psychological. I suggested that he might be able to help. His psychological counselling helped the teenager to find his own inner equilibrium. And he was later able to attend a sixth form college as a boarder. As soon as he did so his parents split up – which was a great relief for him. His parents had constantly told him – separately – that they only stayed together for his sake. He had carried an enormous amount of guilt as a result, guilt that was literally depressing him. Once he was at college, he had no further trouble with poltergeists or depression. Moving out of that poisonous atmosphere was all he needed to feel psychologically, and therefore, psychically, healthy.

Flower Essence for Depression and Suicidal Feelings

Warratah (Bush) – works fast (take every half an hour initially, then three times a day until the depression totally lifts).

Flower Essences for Clearing Entities and Negative Energies in a House

Crystal Clear and Astral Clear (Petal); Alaskan Environmental Set.

Moving House

When moving house it is both good sense and a kindness to those who move in after you, to clear your energies out before you go. To do this you can use sound such as a Tibetan bowl, burn incense or waft the smoke from a smudge stick around the house with a feather, or spray with Crystal Clear.

Exercise: House Clearing

Starting at the top of the house, do each room in turn. It is usual to do the four directions – North, South, East and West – and then clear the whole room especially the corners and the fireplace. Remember to do attics, cupboards, corridors and stairs.

Then visualize bright white light coming in to fill the whole house, re-energizing it and preparing it for its new occupants.

Check that you are taking all your energy with you. Any regrets at leaving, or particularly strong memories or desires, may mean that you leave a small piece of yourself behind. So, before leaving for the last time, check that your aura is intact and consciously walk out of the door 'in one piece'.

Moving too many mementos and 'rubbish' with you is counter-productive so do your clearing out before you leave. Do not take papers, etc, with you to 'sort out later', and any items you are taking that have particularly strong memories attached could benefit from a spray with Crystal Clear.

When moving in, treat the whole house in the same way – preferably before your belongings are moved in – to clear out any energy left behind. (It can also be useful to have the house checked and treated for geopathic stress if appropriate.)

Psychic Protection in the Workplace

Creating a safe working environment is just as important at the psychic level as at the physical. If you have to share an office or other working space, then you can create a pyramid to protect your own personal space – you do not have to be present to 'erect' the pyramid, you can visualize it before you get to work and cleanse it after work. You can also picture your office or working space filled with transmutative golden light. You will also find that potted plants – especially spider plants – help considerably in keeping the work area fresh and clear, as do crystals and flower essences.

If you are in a place where psychic protection and space clearing would be thought 'weird' – creating problems for you – then you can put Crystal Clear (Petal) in a plant mister and spray your plants at regular intervals. If the mist spills over into your personal space, then so much the better (and you may like to position a plant to ensure that it does). Adding a little essential oil of lavender creates a more relaxing atmosphere.

The ideal plant for a working environment is a spider plant as this soaks up negative energy. If you have a computer in your working environment, then a Cereus Peruvianus cactus will absorb the electro-magnetic radiation this puts out.

If you work with people, and especially if you have a great deal of negative or aggressive energy around, then you can put a glass bowl of water in the room to absorb this energy. Make sure you change the water daily. You can add glass marbles or crystals to the water to make it look more attractive. Moving water is also helpful as it creates negative ions, and you may like to have a small indoor fountain in the room – into which you can place crystals. Large, purpose-made plant stands with a water fountain can help if you have a large space to cleanse (see Appendix) and these can be attractive features in your home.

If you are a therapist or healer, then spraying with **Crystal Clear** after each session will greatly enhance your working atmosphere. Nothing will be left to be absorbed by the next person, and you will not take anything away with you. You may also find spraying your patient or client helpful if there has been an emotional catharsis. (If you use a bowl of water in the room to collect negative energies, then remember to change this whenever there have been particularly strong emotions around.)

Crystals also help in the workplace (see page 88). A large piece of **obsidian** or **smoky quartz** will absorb negative energies, as will amber (but remember to cleanse them regularly). A piece of **rose quartz** and an **amethyst** will help to create a more harmonious atmosphere and are especially helpful where there is conflict.

Space Protection via Plant Energy Essences, Crystals and Sound

Plants have a particularly beneficial energy in negative energy situations. Spider plants absorb negative energies; they seem to thrive on them. They are especially useful in absorbing negative emotional energy. Cereus Peruvianus cactus absorbs electromagnetic energy and should be placed near televisions, computers or other electrical equipment. Smudging with sagebrush is a time-honoured method of space clearing. Purpose-made smudge sticks can be purchased which are burnt and the smoke wafted around the room – sometimes with a special feather kept for the purpose. A few dried leaves of sage on an open fire can have the same effect. Incense or joss-sticks often use plant material and burning these helps to clear the air in more ways than one.

Flower essences work on more subtle levels to clear the energies of a place. The Alaskan Flower Essences include a special set of environmental protection and cleansing essences, as do many other essence sets. The Alaskan combination **Grass of Parnassus**, **Solstice Storm** and **Sweetgrass** will clear your immediate environment. Space-clearing essences, such as **Crystal Clear** (Petal) will disperse thought forms, negative energies and emotional residues. **Astral Clear** (Petal), which clears entities, is best dispersed through placing a few drops on the water of an essential oil burner heated by a candle. If radiation is a problem, then a bottle of **T.1** essence (Korte) can be left standing in the room or a drop put on a crystal (do not take internally) – but **T.1** should be kept away from other flower essences as it can absorb their energies and neutralize them. **Ti** (Aloha, FES) lifts a curse from a place. The Aloha essence **Kamani** protects the sanctity of a place from negative energies, and the

Alaskan essences **Purification** and **Guardian** cleanse and keep the energies protected.

Sound can also be used to clear the residues in your space. Beating a drum, shaking a rattle or playing a Tibetan bowl will quickly disperse energies. When working in this way, be sure to do the four directions (North, South, East and West) and all the corners of a room. If using a Tibetan bowl, the note of the bowl changes as the energy clears. Either a drum or a bowl can sound 'flat' as though the sound is being absorbed until the energies clear.

Placing crystals around the room is also helpful in absorbing or transmuting energies. A piece of **smoky quartz** or **black obsidian** will absorb negative energy. **Amber** and **bloodstone** cleanse and transmute energies. **Black tourmaline**, **jet**, **fluorite** and **black-jade** return energies that have been directed towards you back to their source – as does a mirror placed facing the direction from which psychic attack emanates. **Rose quartz** and amethyst attract protective, loving energies. **Turquoise** clears environmental pollutants and **malachite** is helpful if you live near a nuclear power station. (You can dowse the correct spot of your crystals using a pendulum.)

The following case histories come from the work of David Eastoe, creator of Crystal Clear (Petal) and Astral Clear, and demonstrate the range of situations in which these essences can be used. As David says: 'Researching how to disperse accumulated "psychic pollution" revealed effective means of clearance using plant energy essences, crystals and sound. Further development and practical field tests resulted in the creation of two user friendly products, **Crystal Clear** and **Astral Clear**'.

CASE HISTORY: AN OLD FARMHOUSE IN SOMERSET

This was not a happy place, and many years of emotional turmoil culminated in an attempted suicide and a family close to total despair.

In the kitchen and living room, the space was dark and gloomy, depressing even though building work had made it look good physically. I sprayed the place with liberal doses of Crystal Clear, which not only lightened the psychic atmosphere a great deal, but it also allowed more physical light into the building – as if a hidden curtain had been drawn. This was experienced by the lady of the house, even though she professed no psychic sensitivity. The place felt welcoming for the first time in years!

The goat shed was another difficult area. It was regarded as 'haunted' and was the scene of the attempted suicide of the man of the house. The children refused to enter, day or night. Use of Crystal Clear and Astral Clear rendered the place harmless, and the kids now play in there and even sleep overnight in summer. A happy vibe at last!

CASE HISTORY: EARTH ENERGY CLEARANCE

Experimenting with plant essences to clear landscape energies, I took on a challenge. Once again in Somerset, this time along an infamous stretch of the Fosse Way, the old Roman Road, the dark and spooky scene of many ghastly road accidents, ghost stories and a general psychic blackspot. Taking an area about half a mile square, and introducing powerful plant energy essences to specifically dowsed points in the landscape, it was interesting to note that I was met by hostility and even threats as I legally walked public footpaths. The energy of the people seemed to have been badly affected by the surroundings. There were many large ferocious hounds and tall fences, fear was tangible in the air. As the plant energy opened an energy vortex and

began the clearing, I saw lots of 'stuff' being sucked away, including a lot of human blood. I felt the site to have been a battlefield, a fact later confirmed. After the clearance, that one little piece felt a fair bit lighter, even a couple of years later, although it would probably take a whole army of 'cleaners' to sort out the whole area.

If David had not cleared that piece of land, people visiting it could well have picked up the angry and negative energies around it – as its inhabitants clearly had. This could have manifested as faintness or coldness, or a sudden argument with their companion. Not everyone would recognize that it was the energy of a place that made them feel ill or angry.

It is possible to be badly affected by the energies on the site of an old battle – even when it is unknown as a battlefield. Sometimes the feelings picked up psychically masquerade as something entirely *other*. Indeed, there are people who have visited such sites and tuned into entities still there, or simply into the energies of the place, and then reported past lives based on what they picked up (which is not to say that other people have not been reminded of a genuine past life at such spots). Visitors have been haunted by nightmares of the battle, or carried away the psychic energy of the place – leading to a depression that was most probably not even recognized as linking to that visit. The same thing happens at old grave sites and wherever there have been ancient dramas or traumas leaving a psychic residue behind.

For sensitive people, standing on a ley line or place where geopathic stress is strong will bring about similar symptoms. For this reason, it is always worth checking the earth energies before meditating or 'working' at a sacred site. Such sites hold the energy imprint of all that has gone before and you cannot assume that it was all 'good'.

And finally, a case history from David which reminds us that some people may not want to have the energy around them cleared.

CASE HISTORY: PREFERRING 'SHADOWS' TO 'LIGHT'

Working as a musician in a hippy café, I would use Crystal Clear to cleanse the space first, so I could better enjoy an otherwise rather seedy atmosphere. The café often hosted young travellers and one such lady was present as I dowsed the energy and sprayed Crystal Clear. She displayed open hostility to my action, and once the space was clear, moved her seat to a side room which was still 'in the shadows', where she sat and glowered at me for a while before leaving. She taught me something, some people feel more comfortable in the shadows, where they can presumably go on hiding.

David's last comment reminded me of a similar incident with **Crystal Clear**. I had gone to the London Book Fair to meet a publisher. The energy at Olympia was thick and turgid. A blend of the hundreds of people there and the thousands of ideas that were flying out from the books on display. Feeling unable to breathe, and aware that the stall of a 'spiritual' book publisher should not be so affected, I sprayed **Crystal Clear** liberally around the stand. As it landed on the publisher, he jumped violently and shrieked, rubbing at himself as though scalded. I thought this rather strange as the rest of the people on the stand were commenting on how much better it felt but I paid it no further attention.

Some time later, I was on the receiving end of a particular nasty attack via the telephone from that same publisher – an attack which left a foetid odour hovering around the corner of the room where the phone is, rather like extremely stale socks. My partner dealt with that by putting Andreas Korte's T.1 essence on the phone, and we had no more trouble. But when I recalled the incident with the **Crystal Clear** my partner commented that it must have been like applying garlic to a vampire!

I always spray **Crystal Clear** in my regression room or in workshops as a completion to past-life or other work that releases negative emotions or energies. I also use it after we have done tie-cutting of any kind. It clears the air miraculously. People often ask to be sprayed all over as they can feel the change of energy instantaneously. Nevertheless, I have noticed that a few people find the use of **Crystal Clear** unpleasant. These people usually have more work to do — which can include soul retrieval, detaching an entity from their aura, or lifting a curse or vow that has been placed on them. But, as David Eastoe says, it can also indicate someone who is more comfortable remaining the way they are.

Soul Retrieval

Regaining a part of the soul (or spiritual energy) that has become detached through trauma, strong emotion, etc, in the present or a past life.

I have noticed that a spray bottle of **Crystal Clear**, when left standing in a room, can quickly absorb negative energies and may smell 'musty' when sprayed. If this happens, empty the contents away and boil the spray bottle before refilling.

Protecting Your Computer

It is not only 'thoughts on the ether' that are a vehicle for psychic invasion, or attack. Technology offers a fast route right into your home or workplace. Technology gives problems in other ways, too, generating electromagnetic stress for instance, as we have seen. But there is another danger. Your own energy might well interact incompatibly with that of your computer, particularly if you are psychic.

Computers put out a strong energy field. Even the best screened machine creates a wide electromagnetic disturbance. A field with which your own energies will interact. Electromagnetic pollution has been shown to adversely affect physical and psychological health. You can protect your energies by the use of flower essences such as **Yarrow Special Formula** (FES and other suppliers). You can wear purpose-made devices and crystals around your neck to protect yourself. A **fluorite** crystal or a Cereus Peruvianus cactus can be placed near the computer to absorb the emanations. But you may still find yourself feeling quite ill at the end of a day at the keyboard. Even a few minutes can drain the energy of someone who is sensitive. Your immune system can suffer and you may find yourself prone to fatigue, loss of concentration, anxiety, allergies, inflammation and infections at all levels. Fortunately Quantum Magnetica (see Appendix) have a device that counteracts this, as do other suppliers.

Notwithstanding, whilst electromagnetic stress can create difficulties for human beings, the reverse is also true. Electrical and electronic equipment is particularly sensitive to psychic vibrations – and to the energy human beings put out. You may have noticed that when you are having a particularly 'bad computer day' and become more and more stressed, the machine responds in kind. This is not

simply due to hitting the wrong keys. The computer is interacting with your energy – and feels like it is being psychically attacked. So, metaphorically speaking, it fights back. To get the best out of computer and operator, you need to cleanse and protect your energies and those generated by the computer. The following case study is taken from my own experience.

CASE HISTORY: REVOLUTIONIZING A COMPUTER RELATIONSHIP

When my new computer persistently crashed, I took it back time and time again. Everything was checked. The software was reloaded. A 'magic box' was installed to deal with power surges, but still it malfunctioned. Eventually the engineer said in exasperation: 'The only thing I can think of is that you have a ghost.' 'No, I've dealt with those,' I replied. 'Well, what about geopathics. Are there any ley lines around?' 'I've dealt with that too,' I replied. 'We have a Quantum Life machine to sort those out and it has been checked out by dowsers and psychics.' 'It must be you, then, have you thought of screening the computer from your energies? Psychics are a menace around computers.' So home I went to put an electrostatic screen on the computer – along with a fluorite crystal and a statue of Thoth, ancient Egyptian patron of writers, for good measure. I took my Yarrow essence and wore a special disc around my neck. The computer still crashed. And I had a persistent headache, permanent insomnia and no concentration or creativity at all. With three books to write, something had to be done.

Then I met Victor Sims, a computer wizard with a special interest in complementary therapies. I mentioned my difficulties to him and he introduced me to Computer Clear. It revolutionized my relationship with my computer.

Computer Clear is a computer programme that 'generates digitally encoded Homeopathic and Complementary Medicine matrices which resonate with the wavelike behaviour of the body's energy stems.' In other words, it treats the computer and the user on a subtle, homeopathic level. This allows the body to restore its own healing mechanisms and counteract electromagnetic pollution. Because it works on such subtle levels, it gives psychic protection as well as physical – for both the operator and the machine. The only time my computer has crashed since using Computer Clear is when I forgot to switch the programme on (fortunately the latest programme comes on automatically), and I can use the computer for long hours at a stretch without feeling physical or mental stress.

Now, just to be on the safe side, I also wear an Aum computer protection device. I find I can think more clearly with it.

Flower Essences for Computer Stress

Yarrow Special Formula (FES and others); Oriba (Arame).

EIGHT

PSYCHIC PROTECTION and the Spiritual Life

Just because you are walking a spiritual path or doing spir-itual work of one kind or another – meditation, healing and the like – it does not mean you are well protected. You are, if you ensure that your aura is strong and you call on your guides and guardians – and if you have consciously created a safe space before you commenced work. But it is a paradoxical truth that, without protection, as you expand your awareness and reach the highest states of consciousness, so you can become more open to psychic invasion and leeching of your energy. As we have seen, opening up your chakras can be like lighting a beacon to attract attention from the different planes of being – and not all that attention will be welcome and beneficial. It is when you are opening up psychically or learning meditation or healing that you most need psychic protection.

Equally, it is most unwise to assume that, when you are working in a group, the space will be cleared and protected for you and that all the group will be working on the highest vibration. You have the responsibility for your own protection.

The Higher Self

One of the most effective ways to defend yourself during spiritual work is to be in touch with your Higher Self. As this is the part of your consciousness that vibrates at a higher rate than your physical body, it resonates with the spiritual realms. Being enfolded in your Higher Self provides natural protection. Embodying the Higher Self even more so.

Higher Self

The part of your consciousness that is eternal, divine and all-seeing. Your Higher Self functions beyond the confines of the earth plane and can therefore guide and guard you from a place of wisdom.

The aim of most spiritual practices is to raise your consciousness, to be in touch with the divine. If you can raise your physical vibrations sufficiently to embody your Higher Self, to bring more of it down to function on the earth plane, then you will automatically be in touch with the spiritual level.

The following exercise should be taped, with appropriate pauses, or be read aloud by a friend giving you plenty of time to carry out each instruction. Do not try to hurry it as it is much more likely to work when you are deeply relaxed.

Exercise: Embodying the Higher Self

Settle yourself down in a comfortable place where you will not be disturbed. Breathe gently and easily. Raise and lower your eyelids ten times, then allow your eyes to remain closed. Your eyelids will feel relaxed and pleasantly heavy.

Raise your eyebrows high and stretch your whole face. Then relax and let go. Let the relaxed feeling from your eyelids travel slowly up your forehead and across your scalp, and then through all your facial muscles. Smile as widely as you can, and then allow your face to relax.

Now lift your shoulders up to your ears and let go. Allow the relaxed feeling to flow on down through your body. Take a big breath and sigh out any tension you may be feeling. Let your chest and back relax and soften.

Clench your fists and then let them relax on your thighs. Allow the sense of relaxation that is passing through your body to go down your arms. Any tension that is left will simply drip out of your fingertips and trickle down to the earth.

Pull your belly in, breathing deeply. Then let all your breath out and count to ten. Allow your lower back and abdomen to feel warm and relaxed.

Let the feeling of relaxation go on down through your thighs and knees, flowing down your legs to your feet. Scrunch up your toes and then let them relax. If there is any tension left in your body at all, allow this to drain out of your feet.

You will now be feeling comfortably warm and peaceful. Spend a few moments enjoying this feeling of total relaxation. You will remain mentally alert but physically relaxed.

When you are ready, take your awareness to your heart and your higher heart chakras (you can touch them to focus your attention there). Allow them to unfold, opening like the petals of a flower. Then take your attention up to the crown chakra at the top of your head. Allow this chakra to fully open. The chakras above your head will begin to open and you may feel like there is a string pulling you up; allow yourself to go with this feeling. Consciously allow your vibrations to rise, to reach the highest possible level.

Then, when you are ready, invite your Higher Self to move down through these chakras until your Higher Self fills your crown chakra.

From the crown chakra, feel your Higher Self enfold your whole body. Experience the love that your Higher Self has for you. Bask in its warmth, draw that love deep into your being.

Spend time with your Higher Self, welcoming it, learning to trust and feeling safe. (Take as long as you need at this point.)

Then, when you are ready, bring your Higher Self into your heart chakras. Embody your Higher Self at the centre of your being. Enfold your Higher Self within your heart so that it is always accessible to you. Feel how different your body is when you embody your Higher Self. How much more protected you feel, how much more aware you are at a spiritual level as your vibrations are raised by the embodiment of your Higher Self.

When you are ready to end the exercise, ask your Higher Self to remain with you, safely within your heart, and enfold your Higher Self within the heart chakras as you close them gently inwards.

Then carefully close down the chakras above your head, letting them fold in on themselves like flowers closing for the night. Close the crown chakra and make sure that your earth chakra is open and holding you firmly in incarnation. Check that your grounding cord is in place, linking you deep into the earth.

Then, slowly, bring your attention back to your physical body and the room around you. Move around a little, have a stretch and pull your aura into a comfortable distance around yourself (use your hands if you cannot yet do this mentally). Crystallize the outside of your aura to protect yourself.

It may take you one or two tries before this works but persevere. Many people find that holding a crystal (**selenite** is excellent) in their hand aids the process and you then have the crystal as a tangible reminder.

Flower Essences for Higher Self Contact
Bromelia 2 (Arare); Angelsword (Bush); Higher Self (Korte); Jacob's Ladder, Tundra Rose, White Violet, Brazilian Amethyst and Moldavite (Alaskan); Nawpaka-Kahaki (Aloha).

Crystals for Higher Self Contact
Selenite; carnelian; moldavite; muscovite; quartz; watermelon tourmaline; valentinite.

Meditation and Altered States of Consciousness

For many people their first experience of spiritual opening up occurs in meditation or during self-help tapes that teach self-hypnosis, visualization or affirmations. Meditation can be extremely therapeutic, if done properly. The Bush essence **Meditation** helps you to reach the highest possible level of consciousness during your meditation and to open to the spiritual realms.

It can, however, be disconcerting to find that, when you first begin meditation, rather than having a sublime experience, the effect is really rather nasty. Leering and threatening faces can appear, a sense of deep evil may pervade the air, or a drastic drop in temperature may occur. You may experience racking sobs and traumatic emotional states. Far from feeling safe and protected, you feel vulnerable and under threat. This is partly because you need to learn to navigate past the lower astral level when you open up your awareness. It may also be due in part to your own unconscious and neglected emotional 'baggage' rising up into awareness. Dealing with such 'baggage' is an essential part of psychic protection but one which usually needs the assistance of a trained counsellor or therapist.

Face Clearing

If you use psychic protection essences and the techniques in this book, you should not have too much trouble when beginning meditation as long as you remember to take your vibrations up to their highest levels before you set off, and to keep your base chakra open to help you ground the experience. As thought takes form, and intention propels you on your way, affirming to yourself that you are safe and well-protected and that you will touch only the highest possible spiritual planes is usually enough to get you past the lower astral plane (which can feel quite scary for a few moments but passes quickly). If, however, you are unfortunate enough to attract the unwanted attention of denizens of this realm you can use the power of your mind to bypass them. You can literally 'rub them out' using a laser light eraser or even a bucket of old-fashioned whitewash to obliterate them.

Exercise: Laser Light Eraser

Imagine that you are holding in your hand a long, slim wand of light. At the push of a button, the wand sends out a shaft of laser light that instantaneously and harmlessly erases all it comes into contact with.

The Laser Light Eraser can also be used to clear thought forms and emotional residues.

Hidden Treasure

However, do not be too quick to erase all such faces, or the animals or 'part faces' that may appear. Some of them may well have gifts in disguise for you. It is not unusual for guides or other helpers to present themselves in this way – say, a disembodied eye first. Whilst it can be disconcerting to see an eye looking back at you, the whole face may gradually be discerned. If you can slow the faces down (they often appear to be passing you by very fast) and take the time to check them out – from the safety of your psychic protection – you may well find that they are not as frightening as they at first appear. You may well be able to communicate with them. Sometimes the faces want something from you – forgiveness, love or compassion, etc. At times they simply want someone to hear their story. And, all too often, they turn out to be characters in your own inner drama projected 'out there' so that you can see them. If you are inexperienced, it may not be wise to do all this yourself. You could well need help in checking them out – help that you will find in a healing or psychic circle, a properly-run meditation or metaphysical group or with a psychosynthesis or transpersonal counsellor who understands these things.

Doorkeepers

One of the most powerful ways to protect yourself during meditation and other spiritual activities is to get to know your doorkeeper. Everyone has a doorkeeper. Your doorkeeper literally guards your

psychic gateways. These psychic gateways are linked to the chakras and occur at different sites throughout your body. If your psychic gateways are fully functioning, able to open and close at will, then they can prevent anything untoward happening to you during meditation or altered states of consciousness.

Doorkeeper

A guardian spirit or angel who guards the psychic gateways that link you to the unseen world.

Psychic Gateways

Energy centres in the brain and other parts of the body that allow the flow of energy between the physical and etheric bodies and the subtle realms. Properly functioning psychic gateways block out psychic intrusion and prevent psychic possession.

If, for any reason, your psychic gateways are stuck open then you will be open to psychic invasion, attachment, walk-ins and the like. Psychic gateways are likely to become stuck open by excessive meditation or healing practices with no closing down afterwards, or by drug experiences that, literally, 'blow your mind'. If you have taken drugs in the past (including prescribed psychotropic drugs) and experience 'flashbacks' or uncontrolled psychic states, then you may have blown your psychic gateways. Traditional Chinese Acupuncture can help with this condition as can the Aloha flower essence **Paini-Awa'Awa** – rubbed on your head or dispersed through the aura on your hands – or the Bush essences **Fringed Violet** and **Flannel Flower**.

Walk-ins

A rare psychic occurrence where another spirit or being takes over or shares a physical body. Walk-ins can only occur when someone is 'not at home' or deliberately agrees to move out of, or share, their body.

A simple exercise will help you to meet your doorkeeper, after which you can call on your doorkeeper whenever required. Doorkeepers are often to be sensed standing behind you. Rather than actually seeing your doorkeeper, you may have a feeling of hands on your shoulders, a cloak or arms wrapped around you, or a tingling of the scalp.

Exercise: Meeting Your Doorkeeper

Settle yourself quietly in a chair in a place where you will be undisturbed. Let your physical body relax and settle. Breathe gently and bring your attention into yourself. If you have any thoughts that do not belong to this work, let them drift past. Do not focus on them. Take your attention to the top of your head and allow yourself to mentally reach up to the highest possible level. You may well feel that you are being pulled up by a piece of string attached to the top of your head. If your head spins, then take your attention down to your earth chakra, make sure this is open, and then go to the chakra at the base of your spine

and open this. Then take your mind back up to the top of your head and around your shoulders.

When your mind is settled and quiet and you have reached up as high as possible, ask your doorkeeper to make him or herself known to you.

Watch out for any unexplained feelings in or around your body – tingling, touch, movement of air, etc. You may have a mind picture of your doorkeeper or have a sense of someone with you.

Spend as long as you need getting comfortable with your doorkeeper. You may need to agree on a few ground rules for protecting your psychic gateway. If so, negotiate these until you are satisfied that your aims and those of your gatekeeper coincide.

Ask your gatekeeper to show you where your psychic gateways are. Check them out.

If you become aware that your psychic gateways are stuck open, and anyone can access you or move in to influence you, then ask your doorkeeper to help you bring these gateways back under conscious control. (If your psychic gateways have been blown open through psychotropic drugs, place a drop of the Aloha flower essence Paini-Awa'Awa on your head or disperse through the aura on your hands. If they are wide open for any other reason, spray the Bush essences Fringed Violet and Flannel Flower around your aura.)

When you have completed the exercise, make sure that your earth chakra is open and close down the other chakras and your psychic gateways. Then encase your aura in a bubble of light and slowly bring your attention back into the room.

Out-of-body Experiences

Spontaneous out-of-body experiences can occur when you are drowsy, deeply relaxed and opening up psychically or spiritually. Adults often experience them as 'flying dreams'. Children believe they are flying. They can also occur at times of great trauma or sensory deprivation. Conscious out-of-body experiences can also occur during near-death experiences or when running a fever. Suddenly, you find yourself looking down on your physical body from somewhere near the ceiling. Many people report seeing a 'silver cord' that connects them to their body.

Such unexpected journeys can create panic, which does not help when trying to find your way back into your body. But there are people who have learnt to journey out of their body at will, and very much enjoy this process. This is fine so long as you leave your physical body in the care and keeping of your doorkeeper or guardian angel.

Dealing with an Unexpected Out-of-body Experience

Stay calm.

The easiest way to get back to your body when you find yourself outside it is to simply think yourself back. This usually works instantaneously. If it does not, then 'reel yourself in' via the silver cord. Picture this retracting into your body and pulling you back at the same time.

If you find that these experiences are occurring on a regular basis, carrying or wearing a piece of **hematite** will help you to stay in your body. Taking a combination of the Bush flower essences **Fringed violet**, **Crowea** and **Sundew** will also keep you grounded in your body.

CASE HISTORY: THE FLYING BOY

A young man had always experienced 'flying dreams'. As a child he enjoyed these, swooping and diving with glee. Many of his memories of childhood were seen 'from above', as though he had been observing them. As a young man, he would often 'wake up' as he was returning over a factory close to his home – it seemed that he navigated by this landmark. He decided to teach himself to do this at will, following the instructions in a book. At first he found himself in the lower astral realm, not a good place to be. The book gave no suggestions as to protecting himself so he improvized with a ladder taking him to a higher level. He trained himself to 'think past' that level and he ultimately managed to reach the lower spiritual realm. This experience was seductive and addictive. He spent more and more time out of his body, and failed to protect it. As a result, his physical body became enervated and he was afraid of 'something attaching to it'.

He was given a piece of fluorite to keep with him to aid safe passage, together with Mouse Eared Chickweed remedy (Hare) to take regularly three times a day. It was also suggested that he should take a psychic protection essence before journeying – and that he should limit his journeys to one or two a week. He quickly regained his physical energy.

Flower Essences for Out-of-body Experiences

Pyata (Arare) – strengthens spirit cord; Mouse Eared Chickweed (Hare) – safe travel; Sundew and Crowea (Bush) – realigns bodies after.

Crystals for Out-of-body Experiences
Fluorite – shields and aids safe passage; angelite – enhances; hematite – prevents unwanted experiences.

Channelling and Walk-ins

Psychic communication in the last quarter of the twentieth century was characterized by 'channelling', that is obtaining messages from what was often seen as an extra-terrestrial or otherworldly source of spiritual wisdom and inspiration. (In earlier times mediumship, as it was then called, gave communications from 'guides' who had usually, but not always, lived on earth, or from spirits or gods.) The quality of such channellings varies considerably and the best psychic protection is a sense of healthy scepticism and an open mind. A willingness to test out the advice given, rather than slavishly following it, gave a natural defence against its worst excesses. As did a questioning mind.

Unfortunately channelling appeals to the ego. Someone who otherwise feels rather insignificant can, in their eyes and those of beholders, gain kudos by channelling a great spiritual teacher. This is the first pitfall. It can lead to telling people what they want to hear – and sometimes to giving permission for something they would, under other circumstances, never consider – or to offering unrealistic expectations of a miraculously changed life. The other pitfalls centre around the fact that, no matter how evolved the teacher may be, the content of the communication has to pass through the channeller's own mind. The vocabulary, concepts and underlying prejudices of the channeller can 'contaminate' even the best of material. (What comes out of a channeller's mouth (or book) may be a long way from what was originally communicated.)

If a communicator who has been involved in a channelling does not leave, or if a spirit takes over, then a '*walk-in*' is said to have taken place (something which seems to happen much more in the USA than in the UK). Some people willingly share their physical body with another soul or spirit, but there are people who are taken over because their own protection is inadequate. Walk-ins are beyond the scope of this book and need expert handling.

Questions to Ask About Channelling

- What is the source?
- Is this really an evolved being? (Content can be a clue)
- Is this coming from the person's subconscious mind or ego?
- Is it imagination or fantasy?
- Is it coming from the astral level of being? (Tricksters abound at this level)
- Is it wishful thinking, grandiosity, disguised lust or authoritarianism?
- Am I being told what I secretly want to hear?
- Am I in control of this process or am I being controlled or unduly influenced?
- Is this really of value?
- Is this a safe space for channelling to take place?
- Are my energies at their highest and most balanced?
- Do I trust those around me to help me if I get into trouble?

When Not to Channel

If you have not been properly trained, then do not channel. If your energy field is disturbed for any reason, then it is unwise to channel. If the place in which you are channelling is 'unsafe' – that is, the energies are not clean and well protected – it opens you up to psychic invasion. If you yourself are physically ill or low in energy, if you are mentally or emotionally disturbed, or psychically or psychologically unbalanced, then you should not attempt to channel. If you do not know your doorkeeper and guides, if your aura is weak and your psychic gateways wide open, and, most especially, if you do not know who is trying to communicate through you, then it would be sensible to desist. If you feel that someone is 'trying to take over', pull back. If you have taken drugs or alcohol, it can create 'psychic overload' and blow your natural protection (the Aloha essence **Kou** when taken consistently discourages astral possession due to excessive alcohol consumption but alcohol and psychic work do not mix). If the group you are working in feels in any way inharmonious or the recipient is pulling on your energy, then it would not be wise to continue. If you cannot distinguish between your own inner voices and that of a discarnate communicator, then do not channel.

A group always works at the level of its lowest common denominator. You cannot reach a high spiritual level if the group is pulling you down. Equally, if your own energies are under par, then, as like attracts like, you will not be able to reach the spiritual levels. Applying your common sense is the best possible protection for you in such circumstances.

Protection Whilst Channelling

How much protection you will need during channelling depends on how you work. It is essential to raise your vibrations to the highest level. This not only aids the communication but also ensures that you 'by-pass' the lower astral levels. It is also essential to close the link properly afterwards, separating your energy totally from that of the communicator (enclosing yourself in a light bubble helps here).

Some people work at a light level of trance, others at a deep level. Trance is a change in consciousness that enables spiritual communication to take place. It may also involve a spirit or being controlling your physical body to a greater or lesser degree.

Trance

A change in consciousness that enables the everyday mind to step aside and psychic communication to take place.

If you work at a light level, then the communication will probably pass through your aura and you will receive it and pass it on, consciously. You may hear it as a spoken voice or thought, or have an intuition. You may also find that you write or speak without thinking first what you will say. When working at this level, a strong aura and chakras in good working order will protect you. But you may need to work on receiving communications only when it is appropriate to do so – if you are 'stuck open' you will not be able to close down the communication.

If you are one of the people who literally step out of your body and hand it over to the communicator, then you need to know the communicator well – and to trust your doorkeeper implicitly. You also need to ensure that all the communicator's energy leaves afterwards and that you have not picked up anything from the person or persons receiving the channelling.

When you have finished channelling, closing down correctly is essential. (See grounding cord exercise on page 58 and 'close-down' flower essences.) Bringing your vibrations back down to the earth level is vital – a cup of tea and a biscuit have a grounding effect as does doing something practical like gardening or washing up. The chakra shutters exercise on page 52 will help you, but you can deliberately place your hand over a chakra or psychic gateway you feel is still open. Holding a **boji stone** or a piece of hematite stops you feeling 'floaty'. Flower essences will also aid in closing down properly.

Protection Against Unwanted Channelling

- Close your psychic gateways.
- Close and cover your crown chakra, using your hand.
- If necessary, close all your chakras except the root.
- Take the Bush flower essences **Fringed Violet** and **Flannel Flower** or **Red Clover** (FES).

Protection against a Walk-in

Do not attempt to channel or allow a spirit or being in any way to take over your aura or your physical body unless you are fully experienced or are in the hands of a competent, well-trained and sensible teacher.

Flower Essences for Channelling
Channelling (Korte); Green Spider Orchid (Bush); Angelsword (Bush) – distinguishes between 'good' and 'bad' channellings; Red Clover (FES) – evicts an unwelcome communicator; Ti (Aloha and FES) – removes spiritual possession. **Close down:** Fringed Violet and Flannel Flower (Bush).

Crystals for Channelling
Rose-eye agate; angelsite; apophyllite; calcite; channelling quartz; rhodolite. **For grounding:** boji stone; hematite.

Working with Other People

If you are working spiritually with other people, as a healer, reader or counsellor; or if you are working psychotherapeutically, or physically as a masseur, doctor, nurse or carer, then psychic protection will safeguard your energies and promote good health. Many people who work in these fields tend to give too much of themselves, becoming drained in the process. There is an inner belief that, 'I must serve, I must give my all to my clients/patients.' If this is your underlying belief, then the first thing you need to do to protect yourself is change the thought! Using the daily affirmation, 'My energies are protected and I serve my clients from a position of strength and powerful healing energy', will help. You need to say it several times over each day until the message is clear.

Running on Empty

No one can work well if they are exhausted, drained of energy and psychically vulnerable. You may even find that you inadvertently drain energy from your patients or those around you. The Western Australian flower essence **Leafless Orchid** is helpful for people who 'give themselves away' or are suffering from burnout. 'Running on empty' can be counteracted by a **peridot** crystal or essence, Qi Gong, yoga, a long invigorating walk, or a simple breathing exercise.

Exercise: Energy replenisher

Stand with your feet comfortably apart and your knees slightly bent. Keep your back straight. Take your attention down to your feet and feel your connection with the earth. Open the earth chakra beneath your feet.

Then take your attention to the point just below your navel. As you breathe, draw energy right down through your lungs and into that point. (You will need to 'belly breathe', letting your stomach hang out as you breathe in and contract as you breathe out). You may also become aware of energy flowing up your legs and into the same spot which will become hot and energized.

Continue to do this for as long as you can comfortably hold the position, increasing it a little more each day (aim for 15 minutes).

When you are ready to end, stand up straight and place your hands over the spot just below your navel. Picture it being covered and protected so that only you will be able to draw on the energy.

Safeguarding Yourself

There are therapists, healers and other people who pick up everything their client is thinking or feeling. They use this information to guide the process. There are other people (or maybe the same people) who 'clean' the energies from the session through their own body, drawing the energy off their patient or client and passing it into their own energy field. Some people are aware of this process, other people do it automatically and unconsciously. If that energy is not released, then it can become extremely toxic. But, from a protection point of view, it is better to find a different way of empathizing with the client or patient, and of cleansing the energies.

The exercise below only takes a few minutes to do (and can be done on public transport if necessary), but it can protect your energies and allow you to know what your client or patient is feeling.

Exercise: The Psychic Screen

Sit or lie comfortably with your eyes closed. Take your mind all around your aura and check that it is whole. Wrap the outer edges in light, creating a protective space all around yourself.

Then picture a screen a few feet in front of you depending on how close to other people you work (and remind yourself that it is there when you are with your patient or client). This screen is like a giant television screen. It has reflective and protective qualities. It does not allow energies to pass through to reach you, but it does register them so that you can access them. You may be able to read them on the screen, or you may briefly feel the feeling, emotion or disease at a subtle level but you will not hold onto it. The screen has a 'Display' button that allows you to see exactly what is going on.

The screen also has a button marked 'Dustbin Dimension'. If you activate this button, then any negative energies will be sent to another dimension for cleansing and purification. If you need to have the transformed and transmuted energies back, then a 'Return Purified' button will enable this.

The screen also has an 'Erase' button. When you have finished with your client or patient, you can mentally press the erase button and all memory will be lost.

When you work with other people, it can be helpful to create a 'protection ritual' that you follow each morning. You could, for instance, start the day by encasing yourself in a light bubble (see page 35) and then creating a safe space in which to work. (If you still wish to be aware of what is going on with your client or patient, see above.) Many people like to have a bowl of clean water in the room – sometimes supplemented by a crystal – to draw the negative energy into the water. You can also use a large piece of crystal for this purpose. Taking flower essences can be helpful. Putting on a garment, such as an overall or white coat, that is kept specifically for the purpose can be useful (doctors and nurses uniforms were originally for this purpose). Many therapists like to have a blanket or wrap that they keep either for themselves or for their patient. When you have the intention that this wrap will protect your energies, then it works. (Shaking the wrap or washing the 'uniform' cleanses the energies.) Wearing a crystal is also appropriate (but remember to clean it afterwards).

Cleaning and Dispersing Energies

As the 'dustbin dimensions' are so good at cleaning energies, it can be useful to have a 'psychic hoover' in one corner of your therapy room. It only takes a few minutes to visualize this hoovering up any negative energies and dumping them into the dustbin dimension for transmutation. Ask that it will be there whenever you conduct a session.

Spraying with **Crystal Clear** then quickly completes the energy cleansing.

Closing a Session

One of the problems that many therapists or healers encounter is 'closing the session'. Even when the client reaches the end of the time allotted, getting them out of the door and letting go of their energy and problems can still be difficult. As can overcoming the urge to say, 'Phone me at any time if you have any problems.' Having strong boundaries, together with a good sense of timing, is essential. So too is a 'disentangling' of the energies. I spray my clients and myself with **Crystal Clear**, telling them that it will facilitate the cleansing and releasing of the energies. It is also a signal to me that I have 'finished the session'. It helps to ensure that the client cannot pull on my energies after the session is finished.

If you have problems with boundaries and are aware that you carry your client's problems on, then flower essences and crystals can help you, as can a simple visualization carried out as soon as the door has closed behind them.

Exercise: Disentangling the Energies

Stand in your own quiet space and take a moment consciously to let your client go. Pull back your energies and hand back to your client, or send into the 'Dustbin Dimensions', any energy that belongs to your client. Let your client go into his or her own space, back to where they belong, out of your space.

Then check your aura. Is it way out? Has part of it gone with your client? Is part of your client's aura still entangled with yours? If the answer is yes to any of these questions, bring your own aura back and consciously detach from your client. Then crystallize the edges of your aura to seal your own energy in.

If you are non-visual: run a ***selenite*** *crystal all around your aura and then seal with an auric protection essence.*

CASE HISTORY: CLOSING A GAPING HOLE

A therapist came to me complaining of severe stomach cramps and energy loss whenever he worked with his clients. He 'took on' every nuance of feeling, every physical symptom, each piece of 'dis-ease'. He worked both with bodywork and psychotherapy and was in training for shamanic work. He was exhausted. He said it felt like he had a gaping hole in his stomach. But he also felt that his ability to pick up what his clients were thinking and feeling was what made him a good therapist.

When I did the 'pyramid for protection exercise' with him, he failed to put a floor in. When we looked at his chakras, the solar plexus especially was wide open, vibrating at a fast rate, and could not be closed, but the base chakras too were over-active. As a first-aid measure, I taught him how to cleanse and close his chakras and visualize the holes in his aura repairing themselves.

I suggested to him that he should be with me on a weekend workshop so that we could try different methods of protection, and I could monitor the result. We used flower essences and crystals, which he wore in a pouch around his neck. Gradually we built up a combination that was right for him. One that would allow him to know what his clients were feeling but which protected him from actually taking on the conditions (Leafless Orchid was especially useful). We also found that spraying him with Crystal Clear after he had worked with someone helped to clear his aura – which, seen psychically, would enmesh with his client's aura as he worked. He had to remember to fully take back all of his aura at the close of a session. Spraying with Crystal Clear was a tangible reminder as well as a useful energy clearing.

As I watched him, it became obvious that he also needed a blanket around him to remind him to protect his energies when he worked shamanically. He admitted that he did actually have such a blanket, but that he forgot to wear it. Putting this blanket on also activated his own power – which was considerable.

By the end of the weekend, he was able to protect his energies and still remain aware of what people were going through. On returning to his clients, he said he felt that the gaping hole had been closed, the energy drain plugged, without that being detrimental to his work.

Flower Essences for Working With Others

To protect your energy: Urchin (Pa); Yarrow (FES, Alaskan); Araryba (Arare); Leafless Orchid (West); Hematite and Black Tourmaline (Alaskan). **To create functional boundaries:** White Violet and Monkshood (Alaskan). **To clear:** Crystal Clear (Petal). **When you give too much away:** Bog Asphodel (Bailey).

Crystals for Working With Others

To protect your own energy: Labradorite; Apache Tear; selenite; amber; amethyst; black tourmaline; fluorite. **To absorb negative energy:** Apache Tear; black obsidian; black tourmaline; quartz; flint. **To prevent burn-out:** peridot.

Group Work

Many groups are convened for spiritual purposes. Members of the group may come together once, or on a regular basis. It is not wise to assume that, simply because the group has come together for a 'good' purpose, it will be harmonious and safe. Groups operate at the lowest spiritual denominator and many people will bring 'their own stuff' to the group. How the group interacts is critical for its success – and its safety or otherwise.

There are many reasons why a group may be prone to disharmony and therefore vulnerable to psychic invasion or attack. Within the group itself, there may be jealousies and ego-conflicts that create 'dis-ease'. There may be strong group members who, when other members are psychically open, 'feed' on the energies created. Power struggles are not unknown, especially if the group leadership is weak or inexperienced. A group, such as a workshop or seminar, may have been self-selected – that is, anyone who booked was accepted up to a certain number of people. You cannot always be sure that you will be in harmony with everyone else who has been attracted by the subject. Nor can you necessarily be sure that the group is operating in a safe space.

There are steps, however, that can be taken to link the group together and bring it into harmony, and to create a safe space for the group to work in. Preparing the room with candles and incense makes a good ritual start. **Crystal Clear** (Petal) is a useful tool for preparing a room, cleansing it of the vibrations that were there before. So too are incense sticks or crystals. Rattling or drumming may also be appropriate according to the purpose of the group, as may invoking guardian spirits. There are flower essences, such as **Quaking Grass** (FES) that will bring a group together, blending the individual egos and creating harmony. **Hematite** placed in the centre of the group not only keeps it grounded but also enhances trust.

Working on creating a safe space together is a good way of bringing a group into harmony quickly. Carrying out the pyramid visualization (see page 80) is an excellent start to a group. Sometimes groups like to pray or invoke together, whatever is appropriate to their purpose.

The best protection for you whilst being part of a group is to trust the group and especially the leader (**Violet** is the flower essence that promotes trust). If you feel that the leader is experienced and in control, knowing exactly what is going on and what needs to happen; and the leader demonstrates an ability to handle the group energies and any ego conflicts; then you will feel safe within that group. If you feel that your energies easily become enmeshed in the group, you can take flower essences such as **Leafless Orchid** (West) for protection. If you feel overwhelmed by other people's feelings, **Yarrow** (Alaskan and FES) will help. Wearing a **labradorite** pendant helps to ground the spiritual energies and protect your energies from negativity. If you are leading a group, **Larkspur** (FES) helps you to develop leadership qualities without ego.

When it is time to close the group, the pyramid meditation can be reversed to dismantle the pyramid and to cleanse the energies for the next users of that space. Spraying with Crystal Clear will complete the cleansing.

Flower essences for Groups

Auric Protection, Tall Yellow Top (Bush) – for alienation; Yarrow (FES and Alaskan) – bombardment; Quaking Grass (FES) – group harmony; Violet (FES) – trust; Leaflet Orchid (Western) – susceptibility to others; Moare (Arare) – for group harmony and love.

Crystals for Groups

Hematite; labradorite; apophyllite. In addition: any crystal can be programmed to enhance group harmony.

NINE

PSYCHIC Attachment

There are many different levels and types of psychic attachment. Attachment usually occurs when there is an 'energy gap' or break in a person's auric field that allows an 'outside entity' to hook in and influence that person's thoughts, feelings and behaviour. The 'outside entity' may be a person – alive or dead – a spirit, a thought form, or several other possibilities. At times, it turns out that the apparent 'outside entity' is in fact an inner but unrecognized part of the person.

Psychic attachment occurs at times of trauma and stress, in periods of great emotion (joy as well as sorrow), and whenever there is a space in that person's self or soul. 'Soul loss' occurs when part of someone's life essence leaves. It does not disappear or dissipate, it simply goes somewhere else. If soul retrieval is carried out, that is bringing that part back again, then the person once more becomes whole and the attachment has to let go.

Soul Loss

Soul loss occurs during times of trauma and of joy. A part of the 'life essence' or soul moves away and inhabits another place until it is retrieved. It leaves a psychic energy gap to which things can attach.

At its lightest level someone *other* affects thoughts and beliefs. At a deeper level, the attachment may be from a person, known or unknown, who strongly influences behaviour or emotions. At its most powerful level, psychic possession occurs when a person has no way of controlling their own behaviour because it is being carried out by the spirit or person 'possessing' them. This latter condition is rare and is not always what it seems – it may be that the so-called spirit is actually an inner part of their own psyche.

Spirits in the Bar

In *Return From Tomorrow*, a book on a near-death experience written by American physician George Ritchie soon after the Second World War, the author describes being taken after his death to a bar near the hospital (where he had died from pneumonia — he later 'awoke' to find himself in the morgue). He had a guide with him who showed him that, alongside the living people who were drinking and smoking, there were spirits whose desire for alcohol and nicotine kept them tied to the place. These spirits had not realized they were dead. Whenever anyone put down a beer, or lit up a cigarette, hands would reach out to grab at what was so desperately craved. But to no avail. However, Ritchie also describes seeing spirits slip into unconscious or semi-conscious bodies, taking those bodies over to a greater or lesser degree.

This is a graphic description of one way in which psychic attachment or possession comes about. It is also a vivid portrayal of how strong desire can create what the Tibetan Buddhists call 'the hungry ghosts'. Beings who inhabit the bardo (or astral) levels and who are held there by their cravings. The mind is a powerful thing and, as we shall see, the beliefs it holds can be recreated after death so that they become 'reality'.

Mental Influence

Mental influence occurs when someone, often a parent or teacher, has a particularly strong influence over someone's mind, to such an extent that it modifies behaviour. A parent, for instance, may believe that, 'I know what is best for you', long after the 'child' has reached adulthood. The sheer force of that thought is picked up, and acted on, by the 'child', who may endure mental torture if there is any thought of fighting against that belief. There can be such fear of displeasing that person that, even when personal beliefs conflict, there is no ability to fight against the influence of the other person's beliefs or directions. (The same thing happens in 'brainwashing'.)

Mental influence can also occur from beliefs that you thought you had outgrown, especially the religious or moral teachings imparted in childhood – or indeed in another life. Many people find that they experience guilt whenever they go against the teachings of their Catholic background, no matter how liberated they might believe themselves to be. Such guilt, and the powerful thoughts that surround it, can create the situation in which people find themselves after death. Many 'lost souls' and 'ghosts' as well as astral entities have arrived in the post-death state, often unaware that they were dead, and found themselves in the heaven or hell of their religious indoctrination. Others, who believed in nothing, have found themselves in no-place, nowhere, not knowing where to go. Still others have found themselves living in the same conditions as they had inhabited on earth, but unable to communicate with those around them – as in the example from George Ritchie given above.

Just how powerful the mind can be, and how mental influence can be from our own selves rather than outside influence, is demonstrated by the following story.

CASE HISTORY: HELLFIRE AND ETERNAL DAMNATION

I spent some time with an old friend of mine who was dying. Despite being very ill indeed and in constant pain, Mac could not let go. He had always had a powerful mind with strong beliefs regarding the afterlife and he had chosen not to have treatment for his cancer as he wished, in his own words, to 'go home'. In his view, the spiritual life after death was the real life and he spent many hours talking to his spirit friends. Now, however, he seemed to be afraid to die. Although weighing only five stone, he pulled out his drip and ran amok in the nursing home. He was clearly extremely frightened. A mutual friend who was there treated him with hypnosis and managed to calm him down. He asked for me.

By the time I arrived he was in a coma-like state from drugs and could not articulate his problem. He could, however, respond to suggestions such as, 'Breathe out the fear', so I knew he could hear me. As we had been doing psychic work together for twenty years, I 'tuned into' his mind.

What I saw surprised me. He was surrounded by a ring of hellfire. While he was still able to talk, Mac had told me that he believed his cancer was karma from a former life he had lived as a Jesuit priest (see *The Hades Moon* (Samuel Weiser) and *Deja Who?* (Findhorn Press) for further details) who had forcibly converted many people to his religion. This life had been confirmed years before by someone who hardly knew Mac, and certainly had no previous knowledge of his belief in this Jesuit life. During a past-life regression, she met Mac as a Jesuit priest. She was a frightened small child. 'His eyes,' she kept saying, 'they are burning into my soul. I have to obey.'

Now it seemed that his old belief in eternal damnation and hellfire had regained its hold on him. Nothing I said to him dissuaded him from the view that he was being punished for his former actions – and that that punishment would continue after death. I gave him flower essences to release the fear and anointed him with essential oils for forgiveness, which calmed him. As the power of his mind was so strong, I suggested to him that he should do some healing back in the other life by taking the last rites and receiving God's forgiveness for his perceived sins.

When Mac died a day or two later, I again joined him psychically. He was once more surrounded by the ring of fire. 'Come on Mac,' I said, 'you always wanted to do some fire-walking. Take hold of my hand and we will go together.' As we went towards the flames, they opened out into a path before us, creating an arch of fire which burned off and purified his karma. We reached the beginning of a tunnel of light where his guide waited. I accompanied him up the tunnel but had to turn back at the top. (Interestingly, the picture of his guide, that he had died staring at, fell off the wall and landed face down on the floor at that moment.)

Not long afterwards, Mac communicated through a psychic third party that he was now absolutely fine. He had shed the Jesuit persona and was himself once more.

Mental influence can occur at a conscious or unconscious level. Some people have very powerful minds which they deliberately use to influence someone else (evangelists, gurus and the like frequently develop this power to a high degree). Others have equally powerful minds but are unaware of the thoughts they project 'out there' to other people. Mental influence rarely wishes you actual harm, it is usually directed towards manipulating you to a particular course of action or belief.

CASE HISTORY: 'LOOK AFTER YOUR BROTHER AND SISTER'

A middle-aged man's elderly mother died unexpectedly while he was on holiday. On his return home, she appeared to him and asked him to 'look after his brother and sister', who were also middle aged. She had been a dominant, controlling character whilst alive, with strong principles that she expected her 'children' (as she still saw them) to adhere to. She had had a very strong mental influence over their lives, believing that she knew what was best for all of them. As elder brother he took responsibility for the funeral expenses. Despite the fact that his younger brother had a great deal of money in the bank, the man was prepared to seriously overdraw his bank account to pay for his mother's funeral – putting his business cashflow at risk. For him, and for his family, it was part of 'looking after his brother and sister'. His mother's mental influence had reached beyond death.

Tie cutting, supported with the flower essences Boab (Bush) and Blueberry Pollen (Alaskan) to break ingrained family and mental patterns, helped him release from his mother's mental influence. He sent the funeral bill to the family solicitor to be settled out of the estate.

Flower Essences for Mental Influence

Black-eyed Susan and Boronia (Bush); Lilac, Possession and Obsession (Bailey); Grey Spider Flower (Bush) and Pennyroyal (FES) – for fear of the supernatural; Boab (Bush) and Blueberry Pollen (Alaskan) – for ingrained family patterns.

Psychic Obsession

Psychic obsession is a much more serious form of mental influence. A particular thing, belief, idea, person is all that can be thought about, it totally obsesses. The condition needs the help of a qualified psychotherapist or psychiatrist.

Thought Forms

Thought forms bridge the space between mental influence and psychic attachment. Thought forms are created when people with strong minds concentrate on a particular idea or belief. It is rather like a charismatic actor playing a particularly memorable role in a film. Long after the film has gone, the image of that character remains. People identify with the image, remember it fondly or reject it violently. How often have you read a book, formed a strong impression of how the lead character looks, and then been disappointed when the book was brought to the screen? Or, on the other hand, when have you felt, 'Yes, that is exactly right', when seeing your favourite character portrayed. Your impression was a thought form. If the casting director's thought form matched yours and the actor exactly caught the character, you believe the casting is correct. If it did not, you are deeply disappointed. But, of course, there are probably thousands of thought forms of that particular character around.

In magical working, this ability of the mind to create has always been utilized to bring 'servant beings' into form. Spells and incantations for this purpose abound in occult literature and it could well be that some of these forms are still around – the tomb guardians of ancient Egypt, for example. They no longer serve a purpose, but until someone disperses them, the thought form will continue.

Meeting thought forms, and learning how to control or disperse them, was once a part of spiritual training. Initiates would be shown how to deal with them – and rigorously tested to ensure that the ability became automatic. If you believed in the thought form, it could overcome you. But if you saw it for what it was – an illusion – it was easy to overcome. This can be useful when travelling the astral realms – which are full of thought forms. If you can remember (or re-member) an old ability from another life, then you have a natural aptitude when faced with that task in your present life.

However, we create thought forms everyday. When we have strong desires, we create what we want on the mental level. When we hate, or if we are resentful or jealous, we also create a thought form. Thought forms feed off strong emotional energy. It is that thought form that can attack someone against whom we have a grudge – even if we do not consciously wish it. So, if you become aware of thoughts going out that will do harm, it is as well to neutralize them as quickly as possible.

Having positive, uplifting thoughts is obviously preferable to pessimistic, fearful or negative thoughts. It attracts good things to you. Guarding your own thoughts, creating a 'thought policeman' for yourself, can also be a wise move. The 'thought policeman' will remind you whenever you are getting caught up in creating a thought form that you might prefer not to exist.

Removing your energy, stopping your thoughts, is one way of protecting yourself. As thought forms need energy to feed off, if you take your attention away, the thought forms – either of your own making or those of others – cannot flourish.

The ability to create can be used for protective purposes. Whenever you do one of the exercises in this book, you are creating a thought form. Whenever you call on one of your guardians for protection, you manifest it.

As thought forms are potent beings, they can easily influence the living. They can influence at a mental level through the aura, or become more strongly attached at an emotional level. It is always worth checking out whether an apparent spirit is actually a thought form. Thought forms have no soul, and can therefore be dispersed instantly. Spirits, on the other hand, need moving on into the light. But, as we will see from the following case history, it can be extremely difficult to tell the difference.

CASE HISTORY: OBSESSED WITH SEX

A man in his twenties came to see me. He was psychically open and traumatized following his father's violent murder when he was a teenager. To go to the funeral, which took place in another country, he had had to travel a long distance, at a time when he was tired and vulnerable. He, as he believed, picked up a 'spirit' along the way who was particularly unpleasant with a strong sexual focus. This 'spirit' took over his thoughts and feelings. He became obsessed with sex and sexual fantasies. He began to think he was possessed. He was aware enough to know that it was not him, but he was deeply depressed because he could not clear the spirit.

When I worked with him, I began to wonder whether this was in fact a spirit. Although the 'spirit' communicated, the repertoire was very limited. The same information came over and over, all of it linked to sexual fantasy. When I asked what kind of life the spirit had lived on earth, there was no answer. Somehow, the 'spirit' had no life. I asked the young man to try using a psychic light technique to 'zap' the spirit. It instantly dissolved. It had been a thought form. (My sense was that it came from a book someone had been reading at the airport or on the plane and from the sexual fantasies this had aroused in them. As he was so psychically open, he had absorbed them and they communicated as the thought form.) To complete the work, the young man went back to the time of his father's death and 'collected' the part of his soul that had left during the trauma. Once it was reunited with him, he became a completely different person.

Dispersing Thought Forms

Recognizing that what you are dealing with is a thought form helps you to neutralize it. Knowing your 'enemy' means you no longer fear it. You can laugh at it – laughing dissolves many things. You can disbelieve: 'I know you are not real' dispels the illusion. Thought is after all a powerful weapon. You can also use the laser light wand from page 105.

Flower Essence for Dispersing Thought Forms
Aura Blue (Petal).

Psychic Attachment

Psychic attachment arises when something – a deceased spirit, a living person, or another kind of entity – is able to attach to your aura. This is quite a rare condition and it cannot happen if your aura and your soul are whole. It happens when part of your soul has left – at times of trauma for instance, leaving a 'gap' into which energy can plug. It also happens if your aura has been damaged (see page 33), again leaving a 'hole' into which the energy can slot. Sometimes the spirit who attaches is actually trying to protect you from further damage, but at other times it is an opportunistic spirit who simply happened to spot an opening and popped in. Attachments can also carry over from childhood when an over-protective parent, for instance, does not allow the child to develop autonomy. Part of, or indeed all of, the parent remains attached to the child. As we saw earlier (see page 26), such an attachment may also leave the 'child' open to further attachment when maturity is reached if the parental attachment is not healed.

Attachments are equally divided between people who are still living and those who have departed this life.

Symptoms of Psychic Attachment

- No vitality.
- Energy drained and depleted.
- No creative spark.
- Making life choices that have no connection with what you really want to do.
- Feeling as though you are living out someone else's life plan or beliefs.
- Feeling as though another energy is attached to you.
- Feeling as though someone is looking over your shoulder all the time.
- Change in personality.
- Feelings of helplessness and powerlessness.
- Inability to let go of a parent, child or former partner.

Whilst many attachments come from family members, attachments may be nothing personal to the person experiencing them. You could just have been open and vulnerable at the time they occurred. For example if you were very ill or weak, or traumatized or upset, or were drunk or taking drugs, you would not have been fully present in your body. This leaves a 'gap' into which an attachment can slip. If for any reason your aura had been damaged, then you would have no defence.

Therapist Dawn Robins has found that there are also people who are open to helping with spirit releasement work, who put out the thought that they are available or who find themselves aware of a spirit who is in need of help, but who do not necessarily recognize when something has attached to them. Here again, such an attachment cannot happen unless there is soul loss or a 'holey aura' first.

She says that attachments often show up during tie cutting. Tie cutting is a useful technique that clears the energy between two people (leaving an unconditional love intact). It is rather like the chakra tie cutting on page 54. One person works through imaging and visualization to clear the ties between themselves and another person. It soon becomes apparent that someone, or something, is holding on. That may be the other person with whom you are cutting the ties, but it may be from someone who is holding onto them – attachments often go back through several generations. From a tie-cutting position it is possible to see what is actually 'there' and work from a different level. Dawn finds that dialoguing not only reveals the attachment but also ascertains what is needed to complete the process and allow the attachments to move on. The person may need to let go of feelings of responsibility and guilt or to be released from a promise or vow. On the other hand, it may become apparent that the person doing the cutting is holding on, in which case he or she needs to let go.

Voice Dialogue

A technique where a person (or therapist) intuitively speaks to, and answers for, a psychic attachment or spirit.

A useful ending to a tie cutting (or to the completion of a relationship) is to – mentally or physically – give back everything that is the other person's and take back everything that is yours. You then allow the other person to move back into their own space freed from any expectations, 'oughts and shoulds' that were attached to the relationship.

Such a holding on, or attachment, often arises because of soul loss on one side or the other. During a tie cutting, or other work, it may become apparent that a piece of the soul has left and needs retrieving before the attachment can be dislodged. This is specialized work and should only be attempted by properly trained people.

It may also become apparent that the aura is weak, but that repair cannot be effected until the attachment has been removed. Whilst there are essences and crystals to help with this process, it should be carried out by someone who is competent rather than as a self-help process. It is usually the case that the attachment has so much power that they are not going to let you detach without help from someone who is experienced in the field. The following case histories come from the work of Dawn Robins, who specializes in soul retrieval and psychic attachment.

CASE HISTORY: VOICING THE NEED

'A woman called Claire came to see me two years after her father had died. During his life, Claire and her mother had had a physically, emotionally and mentally abusive time. After he died Claire still felt that he was around and influencing her. It got stronger and affected her personality, creating great difficulties within her marriage. She felt that her friends moved away from her because of the personality change within her.

'I felt quite a difficult personality there when talking to Claire. I asked Claire if she would be happy to try voice dialogue with her father to see if it was him and, if so, why he was still there. She agreed. So I asked a series of questions, which she answered for him. I asked him why he was still there. He said, through Claire, that he was here because there was only darkness out there and he was fearful of letting go. I asked him could he not see the light and he said no, he couldn't. An age came into my head so I asked him what happened at this age and he said "That's when she was born and I was trapped. My freedom was taken away from me and I couldn't leave, I was obliged to stay with that woman so the pair of them trapped me and I was never free again."

'Then I asked him if he recognized any severe soul loss in his life. He said yes, when he was a younger man he had been in a fight and he had killed somebody and he always felt that he would be punished for that. At this point the energy began to change. I asked would he like me to go and see if I could retrieve that part of his soul and he said yes.

'I could then feel the compassion and the love that were there for him. I said to him to feel that love and compassion and very quickly I was "away" and being shown what was necessary in bringing back this life essence of his. As soon as that happened, I asked him: "Can you turn and see the light now and the beings that are there for you." He turned, and then he moved towards it. It was very emotional as he went but before he fully moved into the light, he said to Claire he was sorry for how he'd been but she was a safe haven because he believed he would be punished and go to hell. By staying attached to her he could feel as though he was safe. He also said that the reason he could attach to Claire was that she had also suffered soul loss and therefore there was an opportunity for him to attach to her. To complete the work, I did a soul retrieval for Claire and she has regained her old self.'

CASE HISTORY: A LOVING ATTACHMENT

'Nigel was a gentleman who came to see me. He was an example of an attachment by a living person, not so much from an attack point of view but more from a need to feel secure. Nigel had become aware that his energy was being drained and he had the feeling that some other energy was around him. When we checked it out, I saw a small boy who turned out to be his son. Nigel had recently split up from his wife and the boy had stayed with the mother. Nigel was not allowed access to the boy. They had had a very strong father–son connection and the child was desperate to keep that connection so he had done this at an energetic level. Part of him was there with his father. It turned out to be relatively simple to deal with because the father was a very aware man and was able to show the part of his son that was attached to him what had actually happened. Nigel found ways to break the deadlock about access to his son and also to alert the grandmother – who acted as a security blanket for the boy. Nigel was also aware that he should not have a need of his own to hold the connection with his son, as this would also create an attachment, so he released it and managed to make the boy feel secure by talking to him and telling him he would always be there for him. Slowly that part reintegrated with the boy and he became happier. When I met the boy it was obvious that he was much more whole.'

Whilst appropriate at the time as a way or reassuring his son that he had not lost his father's love and support, the promise that Nigel made to his son might well need to be reworked at some time in the future. Vows to 'always be there for you' are one of the major causes of psychic attachment that reaches over from another life to take hold in the present life, as my own workshop participants and past-life regression clients have demonstrated time after time.

CASE HISTORY: VOWS FROM THE PAST

A participant at one of my past-life workshops, Alice, had a sister who was an alcoholic. Whenever she was in trouble, which was frequently, she would go to her sister for help. She was abusive and disruptive, and very demanding. Alice had recently married, aged 40, and was contemplating having a baby, but was afraid of doing so because of her sister and her needs.

During the workshop, Alice went back into a life where she and her sister had been together as sisters before. Her sister then had been sickly, always ill. Whenever Alice tried to go outside to play, her sister would beg, 'Please don't leave me'. Alice had replied, 'Don't worry, I'll always be here for you'. That vow had carried over into the present life. Alice went back into her past life and changed the promise to: 'I will be here for you in this life but the promise will not carry over into future lives. I have to live my own life then.' Shortly after the workshop, Alice's sister went into treatment for her alcoholism: successfully. Unbeknown to her, at the time of the workshop Alice had already conceived a child, who now has a doting aunt as well as a loving mother.

This was not the end of Alice's story, however. During the workshop we had done a great deal of work on releasing from the past and had used Ti essence (Aloha) to release any attachments or 'curses'. Alice had left saying, 'I feel totally different, I really have left something behind.' We should have taken note of her words! Following the workshop, I stayed on for the night. My hostess became aware during the night that a spirit had stayed behind. Being a determined – and pragmatic – Capricorn, she had fiercely said, 'Oh go away and wait till morning then we'll deal with you.' So, before I could leave, we had to help the gentleman on his way.

He was a strong figure. He told us he had been attached to Alice's family through the female line for generations. Her family was strongly matriarchal, with powerful women and weak men. He said that he had been the 'last strong man' in the family. According to him, he had influenced Alice to stay single and concentrate on her career. He had also been responsible for her interest in the occult – which had begun at an early age. Now that she was married, and pregnant, he wanted to move on.

As he had such a strong mind, I suggested to him that he should ask for someone to be with him who could take him to where the next stage of his journey would begin. Someone came and, after much negotiation, he moved on.

Flower Essences for Psychic Attachment

Ti (Aloha and FES) or Aura Blue (Petal) dispersed into the aura.

Attachment by Inner Figures

We all have 'inner figures', characters that people the world of our psyche. Such figures are also psychic but they occur internally, from within. These figures tend to be the neglected and repressed parts of ourselves, as well as concepts that have been internalized from our parents or from religion, etc. So, for example, we may have a 'good girl' (or boy): a parent-pleasing persona who convincingly plays the small child. Such a persona is totally out of keeping with our adult self and may only emerge when we are with 'daddy' or 'mummy' – depending on whose concept of a 'good girl' it plays out. This persona may also emerge in times of emotional stress or in situations which 'press our button' and bring out that unrecognized part of our character. This kind of inner figure could be seen as a psychic attachment as it unconsciously influences our behaviour.

Not all inner figures are as innocuous as the 'good child'. Shadow figures may include an urban terrorist, the scapegoat or saboteur, a defiant small boy, a murderous youth, the wronged wife, or a jealous harpy. All of which can arise out of the psyche as an attachment and profoundly affect your behaviour. If you are unaware that you have such figures within you, then it can appear as though you have been taken over by something outside yourself.

The most powerful protection against such figures is to know yourself – one of the great dictates of psychic work. The more you know, and accept, the darker corners of your psyche, the less chance there is of one of these figures rising up unexpectedly. Psychotherapy, especially psychosynthesis and transpersonal counselling, help you to meet, and make friends with, these inner figures. In the hands of a skilled therapist, visualization can help you to integrate inner attachments into your wider self as the following case shows.

CASE HISTORY: THE GRUMPY OLD MAN

At the first of a series of my workshops, during a saboteur visualization, a woman got in touch with an inner figure who was having a profound effect on her life. She described him as a 'grumpy old man'. Through dialoguing with him, she found that, originally, he had had her welfare at heart and had tried to be protective of her. But he had become crystallized in his thinking and was now sabotaging her efforts at a relationship. No man was deemed good enough for her and his critical voice whispered in her ear whenever she met with a possible external partner.

Over the next few weeks she worked with this figure, visualizing him and talking to him to see what he needed. Gradually he changed. One day he appeared in a much younger, and more spritely guise, wearing a suit and carrying a bunch of flowers. He had come to woo her. It became clear that, in order to integrate him, she had to perform an 'inner marriage' with him. That is, she had to join her energies to his. She took the Findhorn Flower Essence Spiritual Marriage to facilitate this process. Then she pictured herself going through a marriage ceremony with him and, whilst sealing the union sexually, she saw him being integrated into her self. Soon afterwards she found a new life partner.

Attachment to a Place

Many spirits – of one kind or another – are not so much attached to a person as to a place. Sometimes this is a place they have known and loved – they are a kind of 'ghost' or psychic imprint left behind at the place. At other times they have been 'conjured up' and may take the form of thought forms or other entities. Not all such entities are 'bad' or 'evil', although some may be regarded as such. If a child goes to sleep each night invoking a guardian angel or Jesus, then the thought form of a guardian angel or Jesus may well have been left behind when that child moved. After all, many prayers for children invoke images such as 'Gentle Jesus meek and mild' to 'look upon a little child'.

Problems arise when spirits have a less than pleasant intent or try to become attached to people rather than places. There are times when extremely unpleasant entities have been deliberately invoked — 'black' magic has after all been practised for centuries and it can be difficult when confronted with the remnants of such an invocation as this case history from David Eastoe shows.

CASE HISTORY: DEMONIC ENTITY AT 2 AM

'I once had to sleep in a large bedroom which, as it turned out, was occupied already by a demonic entity of some kind (I didn't stop to ask which kind!). Friends I was with slept across the landing in a different room. I awoke at 2 am feeling the ghastly presence nearby. Reluctantly dragging myself out of bed, I sought a large quartz crystal point, some Astral Clear and a candle. Programming the crystal to disperse the plant essence round the room, I dowsed the best place and set it down. A few minutes later I heard cries from the other room. I went to see what was up and found my friends in a state of excitement. They had woken to see a weird-looking entity leaving my room and heading off downstairs and out the front door. They wanted to know what I was up to! We all slept well after that.'

In such situations, if you do not have **Astral Clear** and a crystal to hand, your best protection is to stay calm and not to be afraid. Fear is what lets such energies attach to your aura. Without the fear to feed on, and without a 'gap' in your energy field, there is nothing to attach to. In such circumstances, you can surround yourself with light, ask your angel of protection to be with you, and leave as soon as possible.

Flower Essence for Psychic Attachment to a Place

Astral Clear (Petal).

Attachment to Objects

Psychic attachment can also occur with objects. In some cases the object is one that was cherished by its former owner, as in the case of jewellery or a book perhaps. In other cases, the attachment has been deliberately done for ritual or magical purposes as this case history from Dawn Robins shows.

CASE HISTORY: THE AFRICAN ARTEFACTS

'A man had been given as a gift a gourd-like object from Africa: a tribal fetish. His girlfriend became aware that, whenever she was near it, she felt there were entities attached to it. He began acting strangely and she was concerned that these entities had attached to him. He ended up in psychiatric care, diagnosed as schizophrenic as the entities had begun talking through him. With my help, his girlfriend was able to work to release these spirits. She spoke to them to ask what they needed. They said that they were guardian spirits who had been attached to the gourd by witch doctors during their ceremonies. When the gourd was brought to England, they had to accompany it. They simply wanted to go back to Africa where they belonged. Having detached them from the gourd, and from the man who was now "hosting" them, the spirits were able to return to guard their tribe – their spiritual function. Once this work had been completed, the man's apparent "schizophrenia" disappeared and he was able to leave hospital.'

Objects like this can also be treated with **Crystal Clear** and **Astral Clear**, and with **Ti** (FES and Aloha) flower essence. If you purchase a piece of secondhand jewellery, it is wise to cleanse it with **Crystal Clear** before wearing it. (You can also spray secondhand clothing with **Crystal Clear** to remove the former owner's vibes.)

Psychic Possession

Psychic possession is a serious condition which requires expert help. In possession, a soul, spirit or emotion takes over to such an extent that it is causal to behaviour. It literally feels like: 'Someone – or something – else is in my body or head'. Such a possession is often diagnosed as a psychiatric condition – and may indeed form part of such a condition. Schizophrenics, for example, or those suffering from multiple personality disorder have no defence against an influx of 'spirits'.

In olden times 'possession' was regarded either as a sign of being favoured by the gods, or was treated by exorcism. All too often the 'evil spirit' that was apparently possessing the person was actually something from within themselves. When it was an actual spirit, it was banished rather than being helped on its way.

Symptoms of Psychic Possession

- Strange look in one or both eyes.
- The person is 'not at home'.
- 'Someone else' may look out of the eyes.
- Conversations in which two voices vie for supremacy.
- Bizarre behaviour, completely out of character.
- Emotionally detached.
- Destructive behaviour.
- Memory loss.

The treatment of psychic possession is outside the scope of this book. As an emergency measure, the flower essence **Ti** (FES or

Aloha) can be dropped onto the crown chakra or **Possession** (Bailey) given three times a day for a month.

Note: When seeking help to deal with psychic possession, ensure that an 'exorcism' will not be performed that merely seeks to banish what is seen as an evil spirit. If the spirit, 'evil' or not, is not moved on properly it will seek out another host.

Flower Essences for Psychic Attachment or Possession

Ti (FES, Aloha) – dispersed into the aura relieves astral possession, lifts curses; Kou (Aloha) – discourages astral possession due to alcohol consumption; Bottlebrush and Mint Bush (Bush) and Fireweed, Golden Corydalis, Greenland Icecap, Labrador Tea, Tidal Forces (Alaskan) – release overwhelm due to life changes and tribulations; Astral Clear and Aura Blue (Petal) – disperse into the aura to clear entities; Possession (Bailey) – overcomes control by others or entity possession; Angelsword (Bush), Black Tourmaline, Covelite, Hematite (Alaskan Gem Essences) release energies from other people.

Crystals for Psychic Attachment

Selenite – detaches entities from the aura; black tourmaline – repels entities; apophyllite – protects during astral travel; rutile – prevents psychic interference by entities; carnelian, chlorite and ruby – help an earth-bound spirit move on.

'Possession' and Chinese Medicine

There is a concept of 'possession' in Chinese medicine which does not specifically refer to entity or spirit possession – although it could do. It is called 'possession' but might perhaps be better described as obsession or 'overwhelm'. It is characterized as 'being overwhelmed with an emotion or by environmental energies' – the theory being that anything which is in the extreme can create this state. 'Possession' can happen on an internal or external level, the inner state being connected with emotions and the outer with the environment. It may relate back to a trauma or it may be connected with the place in which someone lives. If someone is attacked in the street, for instance, the emotion of that experience could possess them. On the other hand, if the area where they were attacked had particularly strong negative energies, then the environmental energies could take them over.

The state of 'possession' is characterized by chaos, felt in the person's pulses (which will be unstable and constantly changing) and exhibited in the person's life and behaviour. A person suffering from 'possession' may be reluctant to look people in the eye and will talk about life being 'difficult'.

Pulses

In Chinese medicine the pulses are 'read' in the same way that a doctor takes your pulse. The pulses reveal a great deal about the state of your organs and your energy balance or imbalance.

This kind of 'possession' can be quite subtle, and may be very specific. For instance, a well-known psychic went to clear a house for a television programme which specialized in dealing with people's problems through clearing the energies in their homes. This particular house was 'very dark'. He moved several spirits on and filled the place with light using his angelic helpers. He was used to protecting himself when he worked, and cleansing his energies afterwards. On his return, however, he gradually became aware that there was 'something in my aura that was adversely affecting me, in other words I had brought something home with me.' He went to see his acupuncturist and was given a treatment which immediately released those energies from his aura.

Acupuncturist Danny Dawson, who was trained in traditional Five Element Acupuncture, explains that this kind of 'possession' is due to deficient Wei Qi (the defensive energy of the body). 'It is rather like having a weak immune system.' Someone who has a strong Wei Qi could go through an experience without suffering harm, but someone with weak Wei Qi could go through a similar experience and be overwhelmed by it, leading to 'possession'. Danny uses the 'Seven Dragons', acupuncture points on the body which are graphically described as 'releasing internal dragons to gobble up the demons'. In other words the meridians (energy channels) are stimulated, releasing the dragon energy that removes the blockages caused by 'inner demons'. The following case study comes from Danny Dawson's work.

CASE HISTORY: THE SEVEN DRAGONS

'A chap came to see me who had had an operation for a cyst on his anus. The operation, which should have been quite minor, had gone badly wrong and had damaged the muscles in this area. He became so consumed, or overwhelmed, by the situation that it dominated his life. He was shaking and crying continuously. The first time I saw him, he was in quite a state. I used the Seven Dragons to clear his energies. By the next week, he was like a completely different person.'

TEN

PSYCHIC Attack

Serious psychic attack occurs when someone sends a concentrated shaft of hatred or ill-will towards you. It is intended to do you harm. But psychic attack can be at a much lighter level when someone inadvertently sends you harmful thoughts. It can also happen when you send such thoughts to another person. We saw in the history of psychic protection how trained magicians in the Egyptian and Ethiopian courts were able to bring the *ka* or soul vehicle of the king to the rival court for punishment.

Black magicians have always sought this kind of power over other people, but you do not need to be a trained magician in order to attack psychically. Nor do you need to have conscious intent, but intent fuels an attack giving it more force. Concentrated, focused will blasts through all but the strongest of psychic protection. Much psychic attack is unwitting simply because the person does not realize the power that thought has.

Psychic attack is common when a relationship breaks up, for instance. The hurt and angry partner tries to get their own back or to stop their partner having another relationship by affecting them – or the new partner – at a psychic level (consciously or otherwise). They sit and brood, they curse and mutter, they initiate legal action that has tremendous venom behind it. They tell all and sundry what a dreadful person their ex-partner is. Such attacks can seriously weaken the immune system of the offending partner, or attract accident or assault through another person, as we shall see. The attack can also spin off onto children, animals or new partners, particularly where it does not make much impression on the intended recipient.

Strangely enough, being closed down, insensitive and 'shut off' can offer you some protection against psychic attack, as can ignorance. Not knowing that there can be such a thing as psychic attack means your belief system is not open to it. But, knowing about psychic attack and not believing in it does not protect you, as many people have found to their cost. Paradoxically, increasing your sensitivity, raising your vibrations and opening your awareness can make you more sensitive to attack – unless you build in automatic protection.

It is a sad fact that psychic and supposedly spiritual organizations can be full of back-biting and conflict. All of which can create psychic attack. The higher someone's consciousness, the more trained their intent, the harder psychic attack can strike. Which is why so many people who come into conflict with gurus or spiritual teachers, yoga instructors, Reiki masters and the like, find themselves under severe psychic attack when they try to leave. The harder they struggle to set themselves free, the greater the hold seems to be. Such 'masters' can take the energy generated and use it to feed the attack. It is much more effective simply to withdraw your energy, refuse to think about it and focus your attention on something positive and happy. Laughing can often disperse such an attempt at control.

Many people teach that love conquers all, and all you need to do is send sufficient love and the situation will be resolved. Experience says that unfortunately this is not always the case. In instances where the psychic attack is inadvertent and unskilled, sending love can work wonders. In the wrong hands, however, love can provide psychic fuel for the battle. It can be picked up, transmuted and thrown back at you as hatred. What does work is to forgive the person who is doing the attack. If you forgive, there is nothing for them to hold onto. Your energy is freed and you can move forward.

People who attack need forgiveness. Psychic attack can so often be unwitting. It can come from someone who is alive or dead –

although it is more usual for the perpetrator to be alive. Where it is from someone who is dead, it is probably carried over from when they were alive, or from another life. They have continued to brood on their grievance but do not intend harm. Sometimes it is personal, sometimes not. The attack may simply be linked to being in a particular place, where the deceased soul lingers and, when a situation arises that reiterates the pain, the 'ghost' attacks.

CASE HISTORY: 'I'LL HAVE NO BABIES IN THIS HOUSE'

My daughter moved into an old lodge cottage when she was pregnant. As the geopathics of the house were bad, I called in a dowser to work on the house. He quietly asked me if I was aware of a spirit in the house: an old woman. At that moment my daughter said: 'Are you talking about the ghost of the old woman?' She had been aware of her since moving in and had actually felt her push her down the stairs a day or two before (fortunately she only fell a few steps). 'The woman who lived here before got pushed down the stairs twice when she was pregnant,' she said.

The dowser tuned into the old woman who said she did not want babies in her house. She had been unable to have any children and 'was not about to have other people's babies bothering her'. The dowser talked to her sympathetically and moved her on her way. After he had attended to the geopathics, the house felt much clearer and there were no more incidents.

As it happened, I knew an old lady of 88 who had lived in the village all her life. One day she told me about visiting the lodge when she was small. It had had a large family living in it, one that she frequently visited. It was a happy place, she told me, and the couple stayed on after their family had grown up. Eventually they both died. Then, a couple moved in. The wife could not have children. They lived there for many years. By the time she died it was a miserable place, no joy there at all. One or two more people moved in but did not stay long. The lodge then stood empty for some years but had been renovated. A single man had moved in and there had been no trouble. But, when he brought his girlfriend to live there ten years later and she became pregnant, things changed. This was the woman who had lived there before my daughter, the one who had been pushed downstairs.

The efficacy of the treatment the dowser gave was proved after my daughter moved out of the house and another pregnant woman moved in. She did not find herself pushed down the stairs. As she is psychically aware, I spoke to her recently and asked how things were. She had had a medium in to check the house as she had become aware of the old woman. The medium told her that the old woman had been very unhappy not to have children. When she had finally left the house (when the dowser moved her on) she had to come to terms with her situation. Now, she sometimes returned to the house to see it filled with children – a situation she now enjoyed. As neither the medium nor the present occupant had heard the original story, their version was useful confirmation.

If you think strongly about someone, especially if you are resentful or angry, then it can create a psychic attack as they may well be harmed by your thoughts or feelings. This is because thoughts are things, they take form and have a life – which is why occult schools have always taught mind-control as part of the curriculum.

There are times when psychic attack, or attachment, comes from previous lives and has been re-activated in the present lifetime. Such an attack can cause psychic interference or severe energy drain and can be difficult to pin down to source. It needs skilled help to release it.

It is also possible to psychically attack yourself. Something happens. You brood. You have negative thoughts. These thoughts turn back onto you, appearing to attack from outside yourself. Similarly, neglected parts of the psyche can rise up to 'attack' you.

Symptoms of Psychic Attack

So, how do you know that you are under psychic attack? All or some of the following are strong indications:

- Total, sudden energy drain.
- Being accident prone.
- Life not working.
- Constant illness.
- Debilitating fatigue.
- Feeling of invasion.
- Feeling of being watched.
- Body pain – sudden and sharp or continuous dull ache.
- Incessant negative thoughts which are not 'yours'.
- Nightmares.
- Fear of being alone.

The following two case histories show just how effective a psychic attack can be in undermining the health and well-being of the recipient, and how persistent psychic attack can be in the hands of someone who knows how to use it.

CASE HISTORY: WHEN LOVE TURNS TO HATE

I was consulted by letter by a woman who had been married to a powerful man who practised shamanism. The relationship had not worked out and he blamed her for all their difficulties. When they split up, he threatened, 'I will get you.' A psychic had warned her that the ME she was suffering from had a psychic cause and that her energy system was so weakened that her body was now 'pre-cancerous'. At my suggestion she went to see my partner who is a complementary doctor.

Once my partner had begun to work with her to build up her immune system and deal with the physical symptoms of the attack, she came to see me. When telling me what her life was like, she commented, 'I seem to have upset everyone. Only the other day a friend physically attacked me over nothing.' The psychic attack seemed to be spinning off in all directions – and coming back at her.

As part of the treatment, I did a tie cutting with her to help her clear the relationship. In the tie cutting her 'guts were hanging out' and her ex-husband appeared as an overwhelmingly powerful figure. We had to put her into a pyramid in order to work. Even when she was protected in the pyramid, she realized she had no protection under her feet and he could reach her through the earth. Eventually, after a long session, we were able to cut the ties with him and protect her. She wore a black tourmaline from then on, and supported this with appropriate flower essences to complete the tie cutting.

This was an interim measure as we realized that he had 'stolen part of her soul'. We called in soul retrieval therapist Dawn Robins and she did some shamanic work in which her power animal, a black panther, crept in unseen to steal back the soul. This strengthened the woman considerably and her physical state improved.

However, her ex-husband continued to try to make her life hell. He began suing for divorce with a large financial settlement for moving out of her house – despite having been married for only a year. She had no money and no job, because of the breakdown in her health, so she could not offer him the compensation he claimed.

She had a car, almost the only possession left to her, which was her pride and joy. It was a flashy sports car and her ex-husband had always enviously referred to it as 'the penis substitute'. One day she gave me and my partner a lift. I got in the back but after a few moments suffered from such overwhelming claustrophobia that I had to shoot out of the car. When I looked at what had happened, I realized that he had cursed the car. The work we had done had protected her, but the 'cursed bit' had been compressed into the back seat – exactly where I sat. When I shot out of the car, I took this out with me. 'That's funny,' she said when I told her, 'This car has been nothing but trouble for the last six months, always going wrong with minor faults.' Although she had been protecting herself, she had not thought to protect the car. I immediately taught her the pentagram protection (see page 75).

Having cleaned my own energies, I thoroughly sprayed the car with Ti essence to lift the curse and Crystal Clear to clear the last remnants of the ex-husband. My client used Ti herself, dispersed into her aura, together with a psychic protection essence, Urchin (Pacific) and one of the original flower essences, Walnut (Bach) to disconnect the link to her ex. To the black tourmaline crystal, to deflect the attack, we added labradorite and selenite to bring in spiritual energies. Her health, and that of the car, improved dramatically.

However, when she went home, she realized that, although she thought she had cleared all trace of her husband out of the house, there were still items around that symbolized the marriage. They had tied a strip of her wedding dress to a tree to symbolize their union. She had to take this down and burn it. She also used a mallet to smash her wedding ring (which she had left in a drawer) and sever the connection. Finally, she was free.

A friend of mine, Alec, encountered psychic attack during a business deal that went wrong. He was, at the time, totally unaware that the man he inadvertently upset had been working with black magic to give himself more power and to aid him to fulfil his ambitions. (This was later confirmed through a third party who knew them both.) Although Alec lived in Scotland, and this 'black magician' lived in Wales, the distance in between was no barrier. Thoughts can of course travel over vast distances.

CASE HISTORY: THE SPIN-OFF

Alec had been involved in a business deal which 'felt wrong'. He became aware that the person involved lacked integrity and that the project was close to being criminal. He quickly extricated himself but it was clear that the other party was extremely angry.

He found that many things in his life began to go wrong, business plans failed and his health was suffering. Aware of the need for protection and knowing that psychic attack can 'bounce off' onto those around you, Alec protected his family, house and car.

However, one of his cats became ill and eventually died. Alec believed that this cat had specifically and quite deliberately taken on the attack to defuse it. As the attack ceased with the cat's death, he also believed the 'black magician' had met the cat in its psychic form – which was powerfully fierce and challenging – and backed down.

Alec said that this experience had actually strengthened him and commented that this man had done him a favour. He pointed out that people who do the darkest things sometimes do good – although not by intention!

There are animals who 'come into incarnation' to carry out tasks like these. They can take on conditions such as attack or illness and 'take them out' with them when they die. Animals, especially cats and dogs, are also quite psychic and aware of unseen things – ghosts and the like. In the olden days, all witches and warlocks had their 'familiar', an animal who worked with them. Ancient Egyptian magicians called on the spirits of the gods to inhabit sacred beings, such as cats, to perform protective magic. Shamans today still have their 'power animals' who can protect them whilst they are in the 'other world'. So it is not surprising that a domestic animal can also appear in its psychic form – something that can be much more challenging than its quiet, apparently docile physical self.

Dealing with Psychic Attack

Psychic attack works on suggestion, fear and weakness. The most potent effects of psychic attack arise not from the perpetrator but from the 'victim's' own mind. An overactive imagination, together with the power of thought, is a fearsome weapon and we often wield it against ourselves. It is far more effective when someone has made a threat against you, or you know you have been cursed, and you feel, 'Oh dear, I am vulnerable and have no protection against this.' Or when you feel that the person concerned is so much stronger than you are. So, one of the most effective defences against psychic attack is to feel invulnerable, invincible and fearless – but not in an egotistical way. It is more a sense of quiet, inner confidence that you are safe. You can practise affirming this, looking yourself straight in the eye (use a mirror) and saying out loud, 'I am safe, invincible and fearless'. You may need to say it for several days before you really believe it, but the secret of affirmations is to 'act as if'. To say it as though you mean it and, one day to your surprise, you will do so. To affirm that you are safe and well-protected is to make it so.

If you are afraid, then you not only open yourself up to psychic attack, but you can also create what you most fear. People who fear the 'supernatural', for instance, can focus on it so much that they appear to be under attack from all kinds of fearsome entities. If they, consciously or unconsciously, believe, for instance, that the tarot is the devil's work, they manifest all kinds of unpleasant incidents after having a tarot reading. It is only by knowing exactly what you really believe, and changing any negative belief patterns that might trip you up, that you can fully protect yourself from this kind of psychic attack.

One way of dealing with psychic attack from another person is to keep a clear field of energy around yourself and to give the other person no energy to use. Withdraw your attention totally from that person and the cause of the grievance. So, you do not talk about them, or even think about them. You keep them out of your mind altogether because they would pick up any negative thoughts from you and 'feed' on it, using it against you.

Another way is to imagine that there is a lead wall between the two of you. As lead does not allow radiation to pass through it, it can act as a block to psychic vibes, particularly poisonous ones. It can absorb the energy of the vibes, rendering them harmless. This is particularly effective if the person who is attacking you is at close quarters – sharing your office, for example. You can surround your desk, or your bed or whatever, with a wide wall of lead and then totally withdraw your energy to inside its protective shield. If the person moves around a lot, pop them inside a (mental) glass belljar or a tin can to contain their energies.

A powerful visualization is to imagine that a mirror is reflecting back at the person what is being directed at you. (You can also put an actual mirror facing the direction where this person is). If you do not want the energy to go flying around, then picture a large pad of absorbent material soaking up the vibes and rendering them harmless.

Wearing a **black tourmaline** crystal around your neck is an effective way of dealing with psychic attack. It deflects and transmutes the energy, blocking it from reaching you. You can also strengthen your aura with auric protection remedies such as **Thrift** (Bailey) which specifically wards off psychic attack.

If you prepare a psychic shield for yourself, you will automatically put it up whenever you sense negative or attacking thoughts coming your way.

Exercise: The Psychic Shield

When you are in a safe space, and fully relaxed, close your eyes and look up to above and between your eyebrows, creating a psychic screen. This is your mind's eye. Build up a picture in your mind's eye of a shield. The shield is silver, with a highly polished mirror finish on the outside to reflect back energies which are coming towards you. You might want to decorate your shield with crystals, feathers, etc. Spend a few moments allowing the shield to form itself. You might find that a sword also forms itself. If so, take this as your protective sword. Affirm to yourself that your shield (and your sword) will always be to hand when you are in need of protection.

Then, when you have finished the exercise, bring your attention firmly back into the room and make sure that your aura is well protected with light.

Practise this visualization a few times before you need it so that your shield (and sword should you have it) will be ready whenever you need it.

The pyramid visualization on page 80 is also an excellent protection.

Phone, Fax or Internet

Communication is easy these days, but this has its drawbacks. We all know those moments when we simply cannot stand the phone ringing again. We have those calls that leave us limp and washed out. But, occasionally, there is something worse. If you find that psychic attack comes to you by phone, fax or Internet, it can be dealt with using Andreas Korte's **T.1** essence (not to be confused with **Ti** essence).

T.1 was made in the Chernobyl nuclear power station – site of the world's worst nuclear power leak. When Andreas and his team left the plant, the guards were amazed to find no trace of radioactivity on them. This was as it should be. Radiation was exactly what the essence was made to combat.

CASE HISTORY: BREAKING THE LINK

When I came under attack via phone and fax, my partner put a bottle of T.1 essence on the incoming phone line socket. He asked that the attack should be routed straight to the heart of the Chernobyl reactor to be burnt up. Interestingly, at this point the perpetrator of the attack, a publisher, decided he would only communicate with me through my agent – which was fine by me!

However, we found that there were times when she had to send copies of his e-mails through to me by fax. The machine would not accept them! Her secretary had to phone me so that I can remove the bottle temporarily. The T.1 does not affect any other incoming messages – it was programmed specifically to deal with the attack from that one source.

T.1 should not be taken internally. It can be placed on an appropriate protective crystal (dark crystals work particularly well), either at the phone input point or by the computer. It is important, however, to keep T.1 separate from any other essences as it sucks the energy out from them and renders them useless.

As thought creates situations, it is not wise to take precautions 'just in case of attack' by phone, fax or Internet. You could try affirming that only loving, kindly communications will reach you. I have long been aware that the telephone system has a connection that takes your call somewhere into deepest space – and leaves it there. You can utilize this technological blip to route any unpleasant calls the same way – dumping them straight into the dustbin dimension for transmutation.

Flower Essences for Psychic Attack

Thrift (Bailey); Fringed Violet (Bush); Angelsword (Bush); Sage (FES); Yarrow (FES, Alaskan); St John's Wort (FES); Garlic (FES); Black Tourmaline (Alaskan); Red Clover (FES); Aura Cleaning (Him); Labradorite (Alaskan); Araryba (Arame); Urchin (Pacific); T.1 (Korte); Guardian (Alaskan). **Fear of psychic attack or the supernatural:** Grey Spider Flower (Bush) and Pennyroyal (FES). **Phobias:** Dog Rose and Grey Spider Flower (bush).

Crystals for Psychic Protection

Black tourmaline; Apache Tear; labradorite; fluorite; amber; amethyst; carnelian (especially with chlorite and amethyst or ruby); smoky quartz.

ELEVEN

YOUR QUESTIONS Answered

Should I help other people who are under psychic attack, attachment or invasion?

No, not unless you have been properly trained. It is all too easy to attract the energies towards yourself. You could suggest a psychic protection essence or crystal as an emergency measure but do not try to 'work' with the energies or entity. People need to do this for themselves, including finding expert help.

Is there a crystal that is particularly effective for psychic attack?

Black tourmaline worn around the neck.

If I don't have a crystal handy, is there anything I can do?

Yes, mentally imagine a mirror (or, even better, put an actual mirror) facing the direction from which the attack is coming so that it turns the attack back to the source. The closer this mirror is to the person who is doing the attacking, the less damage they can do. If the attack is unconscious, then you can place some psychic cotton wool between the person and the mirror to absorb the negative thoughts.

How can I protect my child?

Children may well be unable to protect themselves, especially from the thoughts and feelings of the adults around them. One of the best ways to protect them is to ensure that you are absolutely honest and open, never thinking one thing but saying another. Do not harbour anger and resentment and then deny it as children are aware of such conflicts and it confuses them.

Highly intuitive children are usually aware of 'ghosts' and may well have spirit friends – who will not harm them. If you feel a child needs protection, you can visualize them surrounded by bright white light and ask their angel of protection to be with them. Most children are attracted to crystals and like a 'shaman's pouch' of protective crystals. However, the best protection of all for children is to monitor your own thoughts and feelings.

Is there any other way to strengthen the aura?

Yes, you can go for spiritual healing or Reiki.

How can I quickly protect myself from strong emotions outside myself?

Fold your arms over your solar plexus.

How can I seal my aura quickly?

Cross your ankles and wrists and imagine yourself in a light bubble.

What can I do if I feel I have been cursed?

Use Ti flower essence. A drop or two on the top of the head will clear your aura of ancient banes or inadvertent curses.

How do unwitting curses occur?

People utter curses in the heat of the moment, never thinking that they will linger and have a psychic effect. 'You'll pay for this' is one example.

How can I quickly clean the energies in a room?

Spray with Crystal Clear or burn a joss stick.

What can I do if I feel there is a lost soul hanging around?

It is best to ask for expert help but you can mentally direct the soul towards the helpers who are waiting to take it to the light. Put Astral Clear onto an oil burner and leave the room whilst it takes effect. Take Red Clover internally.

What is the difference between psychic attack, attachment, possession, and mental influence?

Psychic attack is energy directed towards you by another person, or thought form, with the intent of harming you. Or it is the result of your own fears or negative emotions being projected 'out there' onto the world and then, apparently, coming back to attack you through another person. Psychic attack is therefore most usually experienced as an external state. Psychic attack can operate at a conscious or unconscious level.

Psychic attachment occurs when a soul, spirit or thought 'hooks into' your aura and tries to influence you to act in a certain way or feeds off your psychic energy. Spirits can also be attached to objects or places. *Psychic possession* can be a much more serious condition where a soul, spirit or emotion takes over to such an extent that it is causal to your behaviour. Psychic possession is usually experienced as an internal state. No self-help is possible with possession because the person possessing has so much control they are not going to let you detach. You need someone stronger – and this may also be the case with attachment.

Psychic attack, attachment and possession can only take place if soul loss or an energy gap has been created and the etheric body has been weakened.

Mental influence is thoughts or beliefs that are projected towards you, influencing what you do or how you think; or that linger from an earlier belief which you thought you had changed but which still unconsciously affects you. Mental influence does not wish you harm. As this occurs at a mental level you need not be 'lacking' anything, but can nevertheless be wide open and picking up everything that is floating around you. Similarly, the other person may have a very powerful mind. The person with the powerful mind may think they know what is best for you and could still influence you after death as well as before. Psychic obsession is a more serious extension of this condition in which a particular thing is all you can think about, to the point where it totally obsesses you.

Will strengthening my aura help with psychic attachment or possession?

If something is attached or 'possessing' you, it is no good strengthening your aura because you have to detach it first. Psychic attachment or possession cannot occur unless your auric energy is weak, someone else holds a part of you, or you have experienced soul loss. To heal these conditions, you need to regain the part of you that has been lost and detach the part that is not 'yours'. Then you can heal your aura. On the other hand, having a strong aura means that you will not be open to psychic attachment or possession.

Can anyone be psychically attacked?

Possibly. Thought takes form and if it is negative it has to go somewhere. You can experience negative thought forms from someone – even when it is not intended – and if you are feeling bad about something then the two things will resonate.

One way to deal with psychic attack is to be fully aware of your thoughts, emotions and physical being because then you can become aware that 'this isn't mine, I'm picking it up from someone or somewhere else.' You can then take appropriate steps to deal with it.

If people's energies are disturbing me is there anything I can do?

A psychic bell jar is a useful tool. Pop it over them and it will contain their energy – this is also useful when people are talking extremely loudly and are intruding on your thoughts. (It works well on mobile phone users.)

I feel 'floaty' when I meditate

Ensure that your earth and base chakras are open before you begin meditation, and when you feel 'floaty' take your attention to these chakras. Holding a boji stone quickly brings you back into a balanced state.

Can anyone take up channelling?

Probably. But it is wise to have proper training.

Are there circumstances when channelling is unwise?

Yes. If you are ill, emotionally disturbed, physically depleted, psychically or psychologically unbalanced, then channelling is most unwise. It is also unwise to channel in a place where the energies are disturbed for any reason.

Appendix

Where to Go for Help

Judy Hall regrets that she is unable to enter into correspondence with regard to psychic attack or attachment. Assistance may be available from the following:

Association of Professional Astrologers
c/o The Secretary
80 High Street
Wargrave
Berkshire RG10 8DE

David Eastoe
e-mail: eastoe@yahoo.com
Supplier of Crystal Clear and Plant Energy Essences

The College of Psychic Studies
16 Queensberry Place
London SW7 2EB
Tel: 020 7589 3292
Spirit releasement, soul retrieval, healing, workshops and personal advice

The College of Traditional Acupuncture
Leamington Spa
Warwickshire CU31 3LZ
Tel: 01926 422121
Practitioners list for your area in the UK

Danny Dawson and Jo Neary
Tel: 020 8693 5941 (London, UK)
Acupuncture practitioners

The Flower Essence Pharmacy
2007 NE 39th Avenue
Portland
OR 97212
USA
Flower essence suppliers

Steve Graham
Tel: 020 7221 4213
Mobile: 07957 255564
One-to-one entity detachment and healing sessions in London

International Flower Essence Repertoire
Achamore House
Isle of Gigha
Argyll and Bute
Scotland
PA41 7AD
www.ifer.co.uk
email: flower@atlas.co.uk
Flower essence suppliers

National Federation of Spiritual Healers
Old Manor Farm Studio
Church Street
Sunbury on Thames
Middlesex TW16 6RG
Tel: 01932 783164

Paul Speight
Tel: 01685 51947
Supplier of decorative mirrors or plant stands with fountain

World Development Systems Ltd
www.computerclear.com
Supplier of Computer Clear Programme

Anti-electromagnetic and geopathic devices

Noma Ltd
Unit 3
1–16 Hollybrook Road
Upper Shirley
Southampton SO16 6RB
Tel: 01703 770513

Dulwich Health Society
130 Gipsy Hill Road
London SE19 1PL
Tel: 020 8670 5883
Fax: 020 8766 6616

Natural Therapeutics
25 New Road
Spalding
Lincolnshire PE11 1DQ
Tel: 01775 761927
Fax: 01775 761104

Wholistic Research Company
Bright Haven
Robins Lane
Lolworth
Cambridgeshire CB3 8HH
Tel: 01954 780174
Fax: 01954 789409

Manufacturers of Flower Essences and Protective Devices

Aum Himalayan Essences
15e Jaybharat Soc
3rd Road
Khar (W)
Mumbal-52
India
Tel: 9122 648 6819
www.aumhimalaya.com

Flower Essence Manufacturers

Alaskan Flower Essences
Project
PO Box 1369
Homer
Alaska 99603
Tel: 907 235 2188

Aloha Flower Essences
PO Box 2319
Kealakekua
HI 96750
USA
Tel: 808 328 2529

Araretama
Rua Carlos Gomes
100 Perequê-Açu
Ubatuba, SP
Brazil CPE11680-00
Tel: 005 11531 9068
e-mail: araretama@uol.com.br

Australian Bush Flower Essences
89 Oaks Avenue
Dee Why
NSW 2099
Australia
Tel: 02 972 1033

Bailey Flower Essences
7/8 Nelson Road
Ilkley
West Yorkshire LS29 8HH
Tel: 01943 602177

Flower Essence Services
PO Box 1769
Nevada City
CA 95959
USA
Tel: 916 265 9163

Korte Phi Essenz
Alpenstrasse 25
D-78262 Gailingen
Germany
Tel: 49 77 74 7004

Pacific Flower Essences
PO Box 8317
Victoria
BC V8W 3R9
Canada
Tel: 604 384 5560

Second Aid Essences
2 Blackheath Lane
Wonersh
Guildford
Surrey GU5 0PN

Western Australian Bush Essences
PO Box 355
Scarborough
Perth
W Australia 6019
Tel: 09 244 2073

Way of Reincarnation

Judy Hall

Over half the world's population accept reincarnation – they believe they have lived before and will do so again. In the East this is taken for granted, while in the West the belief is rapidly gaining acceptance once again. This comprehensive introduction looks at world thought and contains all the information you need to gain an in-depth knowledge of reincarnation, including:

- *what reincarnation is*
- *its cultural and religious background*
- *how the soul reincarnates*
- *famous people throughout history and their beliefs in reincarnation*
- *the evidence for and against reincarnation.*

Judy Hall is an internationally known author, lecturer and workshop leader and has been a karmic counsellor for 25 years. She has written numerous books on reincarnation and has frequently appeared on radio and television in the UK and the US to discuss the subject.

ISBN: 0 00 710290 9

Way of Natural Magic

Nigel Pennick

Natural magic is a way of working with the vital energy around us, including that which comes from our own awareness and intention. Working with natural magic involves simple but powerful practical techniques that anyone can use to bring more magic into their everyday lives. This comprehensive introduction contains all the information you need to gain an in-depth knowledge of magic including:

- *an explanation of earth, mineral, and plant magic*
- *magic animals and how we can work with them*
- *the power within – the magic of the human body*
- *the magic of the land, of food and drink*
- *natural magic charms, talismans and amulets – what they are and how to make and empower them.*

Nigel Pennick has conducted research on ancient monuments, folk traditions, geomancy and magic for over 25 years. In 1975 he founded the Institute of Geomantic Research. He has worked all over Europe, Canada and the US and is a leading author in this field.

ISBN: 0 7225 4038 8

Way of Crystal Healing

Ronald Bonewitz

From one of the world's leading crystal experts, this is the best introduction available for an easy-to-read and sensible beginners guide to crystals. As well as giving a thorough introduction to the properties and qualities of crystals, this book explores how crystal healing works, and how it can be combined with related therapies such as acupuncture, chakra work and energy healing.

The book stands out for its very grounded, realistic approach. The author believes that many properties are attributed to crystals that they simply can't have, and that much of the information available to the public comes from misinformed sources. This book will give the beginner an honest understanding of the real value of crystals and of how they can develop their personal experiences of working with them.

Ronald Bonewitz originally trained as a geologist specializing in crystal chemistry, and now holds a PhD in Behavioural Science, emphasizing physiological psychology. With a reputation for clarity and integrity, he has given hundreds of crystal courses worldwide and has written several books on crystals.

ISBN: 0 00 710392 1

Way of Tibetan Buddhism

Lama Jampa Thaye

Buddhism is now one of the fastest-growing spiritual practices in the West. Tibetan Buddhism is a branch of Buddhism that places particular emphasis on the teacher–disciple relationship which lies at the heart of the spiritual life. This comprehensive introduction contains all the information you need to gain an in-depth knowledge of Tibetan Buddhism including:

- *what Tibetan Buddhism is and how it developed*
- *an insight into all the basic teachings including Indian, Tibetan and Western practice*
- *the historical background to Buddhism*
- *a summary of the major schools.*

Lama Jampa Thaye (David Stott) is a lecturer in the Religions and Theology Department of Manchester University and a Vajrayana teacher in the Sakya and Kagyu Buddhist traditions, having studied under various masters for over three decades. He is the principal disciple of Karma Thinley Rinpoche, the Director of the Dechen Community in Europe, and the author of a number of books on Buddhism.

ISBN: 0 7225 4017 5